DAVIE COOPER

DAVIE COOPER

TRIBUTE TO A LEGEND

GRAHAM CLARK

MAINSTREAM
PUBLISHING

EDINBURGH AND LONDON

Other titles by the same author:
True Blue (with Davie Cooper)
Football is the Wallace Tradition (with Jock Wallace)
Captain's Log (with Gary McAllister)

PHOTOGRAPH ACKNOWLEDGEMENTS

All photographs are courtesy of the *Daily Record*

Copyright © Graham Clark, 1995

The moral right of the author has been asserted

First published in Great Britain in 1995 by
MAINSTREAM PUBLISHING COMPANY (EDINBURGH) LTD
7 Albany Street
Edinburgh EH1 3UG

ISBN 1 85158 789 6

A catalogue record for this book is available from the British Library

Typeset in Bembo by Litho Link Ltd, Welshpool, Powys, Wales
Printed and bound in Great Britain by Butler & Tanner Ltd, Frome and London

CONTENTS

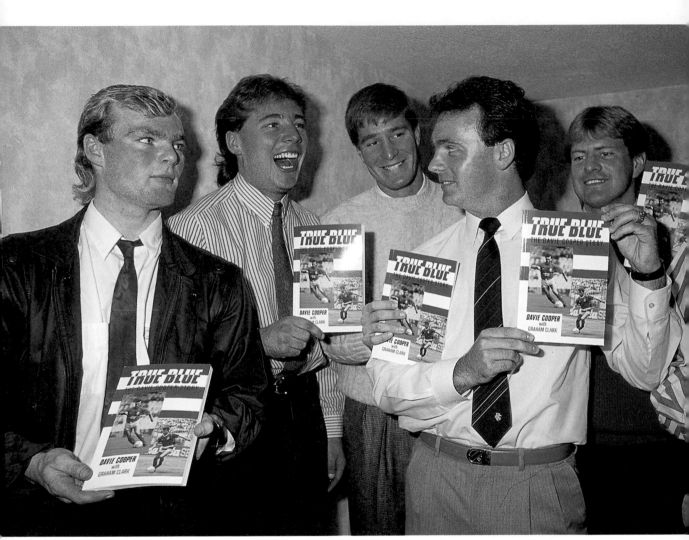

Robert Fleck, Ally McCoist, Richard Gough and Stuart Munro enjoyed a laugh at Davie's expense at the launch of his autobiography *True Blue*.

Davie Cooper – Tribute to a Legend

Davie Cooper. Born 25 February 1956, died 23 March 1995

Davie Cooper's life was spent entertaining millions of people with a talent that was God-given. His death united millions more in a way that has never been seen in Scotland before and may never be seen again.

Football people talk regularly of disaster, catastrophe and even tragedy when they are discussing relegation or a cup final defeat. But Davie's death brought home the real meaning of those words. He was taken from us as he neared the end of a great and glorious playing career and just as he was about to embark on a new chapter in his life. He had great plans for the future. Sadly, he was never allowed to fulfil them and even now it is difficult to quite understand why that should be.

It is somehow incomprehensible that we shall never speak to him or see him again. And even though it is no consolation now I am grateful I had the pleasure of knowing him well. I co-wrote his autobiography *True Blue* back in 1987 and its success owed everything to Davie's popularity. To be honest, I think even he was surprised by the queues of people who turned up at signing sessions around the country. I well remember my sister deciding she would take pity on Davie and me by bringing her children along to a signing session in an Edinburgh shop just in case no one else turned up. She couldn't get near the place because the queue was part of the way along Princes Street. That was a measure of just how well liked and admired Coop was and his untimely death brought all that home again.

The out-pouring of grief from *all* quarters of the community was a staggering testament to Davie's skill, ability and popularity. Clydebank's Kilbowie, Rangers' Ibrox and Motherwell's Fir Park – the three grounds he graced most – were awash with flowers and tributes.

This book is my personal tribute. And the title proved the easiest thing of all to write. *Davie Cooper – Tribute to a Legend*.

Graham Clark

CHAPTER ONE

The Early Years

The basis for Davie Cooper's incredible success lay firmly in a happy, rock-solid upbringing. His mum Jean and dad John added David to a family that already included John who was born three years before.

The two sons could not have been more different. Davie later recalled: 'John and I were complete opposites. He was a right little tearaway who was always getting into mischief whereas I would never do a thing wrong – honest! As I grew older I would hardly go out of the house to play and I have to admit I was more or less a mummy's boy.'

But Coop grew up quickly in Hamilton and by the time he was nine he was hooked on football. And soon after that the honours started flooding in to the Cooper household. When he wasn't picking up silverware of his own then Davie was going to Ibrox to see if Rangers could emulate his feats so that, one way and another, football took a hold on Coop.

When a couple called Bill and Rose McKenzie started a team of their own called Udston United the die was cast. 'It's not too dramatic to say that if they hadn't I don't think I would have continued playing football,' admitted Davie. 'I'm sure I might have drifted away from the game into something else.' Everyone who loves our national game certainly owes a debt to the McKenzies who gave him a flying start to a career that simply got better and better.

Davie continued to progress at Hamilton Avondale and his performances began to attract some serious attention from clubs in all corners of Britain. Coventry City were first to note interest and Crystal Palace were in there too but at the back of Davie's mind was an unsuccessful spell his brother John had had at Hull City. John hated his spell in the south and if it didn't suit big brother there was no way young David was going to try his luck in England. 'I always thought back to John and his trials and tribulations and I never encouraged the English clubs,' he admitted.

Opposite: Davie learned his trade as a printer . . . until football called

Happily, there was enough interest this side of the border to compensate. Davie later recalled:

> I had a trial with Clyde when I scored a goal in a reserve match and then Shawfield manager Stan Anderson immediately offered me £4 a week but while I was flattered I didn't exactly beat a return path to his door. Motherwell, managed at the time by Ian St John, were also quite enthusiastic and the Saint made me an offer. He reckoned I could be farmed out to a junior side because I needed building up. Building up! I had watched John play at that level as well and if that was what was needed to build me up it was thanks but no thanks. John used to get kicked up and down the park and that wasn't for me.

One other problem Davie had to contend with – which affected decisions all through his career – was the fact that he loved Hamilton. He had absolutely no desire to venture far from the Lanarkshire town so even when Clydebank Football Club – which isn't exactly the other end of the earth – became keenest of all he didn't fall over himself or get too excited.

Rangers showed a certain willingness as well but the single-minded Coop took one look at the list of players at Ibrox and wondered to himself when he would ever get a game. 'I know turning them down seems unbelievable to thousands of youngsters around the world but I felt it made sense at the time,' he reasoned.

In an ideal world a Hamilton Accies side who were playing magnificent football and were at the top of the table would have been the perfect choice for the man who got homesick for his pet half-collie Scot when he once left the country on holiday with a pal's family.

But it wasn't an ideal world and at just 18, Davie chucked the game he had grown to love. He simply couldn't find the right team in the right place. Maybe even then he didn't realise just how good he was but fortunately others did. Stuart and Alan Noble, who ran the Avondale team, nearly had apoplexy at the prospect of a talent like that disappearing. The duo contacted Bankies again and put their worst fears to supremo Jack Steedman.

Davie later took up the story:

> Now Jack, as I was to discover, is a very persuasive man who won't take no for an answer. After all, I had already tried one 'no' but Jack came back again even though I wasn't even actively involved in the game. Nothing daunted, he

appeared outside the printing works where I was employed and I thought I should at least do him the courtesy of speaking about it even if the prospect didn't exactly have me bubbling over. So out I went to sit in Jack's car – a big Jaguar – and I was quite impressed. But the thought of continuing my job and then having to make my way to Clydebank for night-time training when I didn't even drive didn't make me terribly enthusiastic. Jack, though, continued his sales pitch as if nothing was going wrong and when you're faced with that kind of enthusiasm it's difficult not to feel wanted. Deep down I knew I was desperately keen to start playing again as well. It would be unfair of me to suggest that Jack then pulled his master-stroke by revealing an envelope with what looked to me like a king's ransom inside . . . but it helped! There was £300 in grubby, used notes which he offered me as a signing-on fee and that, plus the promise of a decent basic wage and more when I worked my way into the first team, left me thinking that maybe it would be worth it after all.

Coop even admitted that he would have signed for Steedman for nothing simply to put his life back on track again. No one could ever accuse Davie of making cash his God. Mind you, I think that admission probably still rankles with Jack! But the Clydebank boss knew then, as he does now, that it was money well spent. Steedman knew a jewel when he saw one and it was all a bit of a double whammy anyway because there's little doubt Jack would have offered even more to net the young Coop. However, both men were happy as Davie took his first genuine steps on the path to greatness.

JACK STEEDMAN

Jack Steedman of Clydebank was Davie Cooper's mentor – from the beginning to the end of his career.

The Kilbowie supremo was the man who managed to persuade a reluctant Coop to enter professional football in the first place.

Such was his admiration for the player that he was thrilled and delighted to take him back to Bankies as he was nearing the last couple of years of his playing days.

Although Davie had intimated he was going to retire at the end of the season he had just signed a deal for a Davie Cooper Soccer School in which he would coach youngsters. He was very into that.

At Clydebank we had a Soccer Skills Scotland project and he was going to front a couple of the courses. He was enjoying doing more and more coaching and, of course, that was what he was doing at Broadwood the day he collapsed. It's criminal what's happened.

But nothing will ever dim Steedman's admiration for the man he took to Kilbowie for £300 and launched on the road to stardom.

He has to be the most talented footballer we've ever had at Clydebank. He was a natural-born talent yet, as a youngster, his brother John had to virtually force him to go out and play.

He was so quiet and shy he didn't want to be involved in football as a kid but once he started it was really the only thing he ever wanted to do. Davie simply wanted to play. He never wanted to get too technical and he wasn't that keen on training in the early days either.

All he wanted was a ball at his feet and a few defenders to make a fool of and he was happy! He had a magnificent spell with us first time round when he helped us to two promotions, but he was always going to move on.

Right up to the minute he did move on he ignored my pleas to work with his right foot. But he was right – he didn't really need it when his left was so good.

When I was playing I liked to keep the ball up a hundred times to show off what skill I had. Davie could have kept it up for three weeks if he had wanted!

I followed his career closely after he left us for Rangers and it was always a pleasure to see him play. Over the years I also saw him mature as a person and from being an introvert he became quite an extrovert. He actually became a totally different individual in the public eye yet he still retained a certain shyness. When Wet Wet Wet wanted him to help launch one of their records he opted out because he wasn't so keen on being up front like that even later in life.

But he could play all right and when the chance came for me to sign him for a second time I didn't hesitate. He gave Bankies some significance when he came back to Kilbowie and he also helped us to avoid relegation.

The legs had maybe gone a bit but nine minutes of Coop was like 90 from someone else. He was never the kind who would battle and scratch the whole game anyway. He didn't need to. Scottish football is full of players who do that and he was above all the commitment and nonsense. He was terrific for us second time around as well as first.

But it was a costly move for Steedman and Bankies as Jack explained with a smile.

I couldn't understand at one point why our telephone bill had gone up so much. Then one day it dawned on me. Davie had sweet-talked Mary, our

kitchen lady, into letting him use the phone to put a line on at the bookies. To be fair, he drank plenty of Mary's tea as well but it was also the one place where he could get to a phone.

Jack could even put up with that, though, because it was Coop who was involved.

One of the last things I asked Davie to do was take the first team for training one night and he was good at that.

But he was especially good with the younger players. He would give the lads who were Celtic fans some real abuse, for instance, and they were never too sure if he meant it or not. But Davie would just be winding them up.

Opposite: Coop with golfer Sam Torrance and boxer Jim Watt

Davie has only one thing in mind when he's got a Celtic scarf . . . wrap it round team-mate and Parkhead fan James Grady's neck!

Posing at Kilbowie on his return to Clydebank

He was really a great example to the youngsters and even now if we're trying to take a young lad to Kilbowie I'll hold Davie up as the greatest example of what can be achieved in the game.

I had hoped he would be with us for the next 20 years at least to help at this club.

Really, I'm just proud to have been associated with him.

So proud, indeed, that Clydebank's new ground will be called 'The Davie Cooper Stadium'.

I am hoping, subject to all the planning details and everything else, that this will be our last season at Kilbowie and then we will move to The Davie Cooper Stadium.

I know he spent a lot of time at Ibrox and also a few years at Motherwell. But to us all here he was always Davie Cooper of Clydebank.

The new stadium, which Steedman desperately hopes will be in operation for the start of the 1996–97 season, will be a fitting tribute to Coop from a club he loved.

CHAPTER TWO

Kilbowie to Ibrox

Clydebank didn't offer the same kind of challenge as Rangers would have done and Coop was quickly doing and showing enough to justify his earlier decision.

Several Bankies' players, such as Andy Roxburgh, were nearing the end of their careers and Davie knew he was heading rapidly in the right direction. But he was making sacrifices along the way. The journey from Hamilton to Clydebank was, to him, a nightmare.

> I hated the routine and it bugged me that I went through it so regularly to get to training which I never enjoyed anyway! But I always knew training was a necessary evil even if all we did for a while was go on endless laps of the Kilbowie track. That was bad enough but those who know the ground will realise you have to pass the Social Club en route and every lap you would look up and see guys inside sipping their pints. I think that must be the definition of frustration.

There was nothing frustrating, though, about his rapid progress to the Bankies first team and one of his earliest games was against Celtic. It was a Parkhead cup clash and for a young Rangers fan it was too good an opportunity to miss.

> Celtic paraded all their big stars including Kenny Dalglish, George Connolly, Harry Hood, Dixie Deans . . . and Danny McGrain. I was in direct opposition to Danny and I'm delighted to say I gave him a hard time. It was, essentially, the first time I had been noticed outside of Clydebank.

But certainly not the last.

Events moved on quickly after that. Bankies won promotion and Davie's first representative honour came along when Scotland manager Willie Ormond selected him for a First and Second Division side for a game against a Highland League Select.

Opposite: He has the whole of Clydebank in his hands

With Bankies team-mate Mike Larnach

Coop was the only Second Division player to be on at the start of that match which gives you some idea of the strides he had made.

Other people now began to sit up and take note. Aston Villa offered Clydebank £65,000 and the Birmingham club's manager Ron Saunders promised Coop *three times* what he was picking up at Kilbowie. 'He seemed to think it would be enough to tempt me but there's more to life than money,' declared Davie.

There was glory for a start. And apart from anything else there was only one club Davie would have signed for . . . Rangers. England was Outer Mongolia to him and that was the bottom line. He ignored the barbed comments about lack of ambition and simply got on with his life.

The Coop moustache . . . hair today, gone tomorrow

Then, almost as if it was pre-ordained, Clydebank drew 'Gers in the quarter-final of the League Cup. It was a dream opportunity for the young Cooper to show the side who had won the treble the previous year what the upstart from the sticks could do.

21

Not content with a moustache, Davie grew a beard. And he left Rangers with a close shave in a drawn-out League Cup tie. This Coop goal stunned big names Colin Jackson, John Hamilton, Tom Forsyth and keeper Peter McCloy.

Opposite: Still early in his career but all left foot

It didn't take me long to find out the hard facts about life at the top. The first game was at Ibrox and two minutes into the match I learned the ground rules according to John Greig.

The man who later became my manager took exactly 120 seconds to let me know he was around. He waded in with the kind of challenge that Jack the Ripper would have been proud of and then, just to rub salt into my wounds, he growled: 'If I get another chance, I'll break your leg.'

There's no doubt about it, Greigy gave you that warm, it's nice-to-be-wanted feeling. Not that he was alone because it seemed to me that he and big Tam Forsyth took it in turns to put me up in the air, wait for me to come down again and then repeat the process.

Despite that 'welcome' to Ibrox Davie scored a late equaliser for Clydebank and then repeated the feat at Kilbowie where the mighty Rangers were once more, embarrassingly, held to a draw.

Before the third match came around, Coop won his first Under-21 cap in Czechoslovakia in a 0–0 draw and others in that side included guys like

23

George Burley, Roy Aitken, John Wark, David Narey, Tommy Burns and Paul Sturrock.

But it was really Coop and Clydebank who were the centre of attention at the time and even more so after yet another draw with Rangers.

Finally, at neutral Firhill, something had to give and it was Bankies who eventually lost a titanic tie 2–1 with, naturally, Coop getting on the scoresheet once more.

Those games, although he didn't realise it at the time, were his stepping stones to a Rangers career. The move was not long in coming.

Jack Steedman, who was on holiday on the south coast of England with his wife Margaret, conducted the negotiations from afar with Willie Waddell. The first I knew of it was when Jock Wallace telephoned asking me to go into Ibrox.

No other club in the world could have enticed me but by then I had weighed everything up and decided I didn't want to take the chance of turning Rangers down for a second time. I liked a gamble but there were times when commonsense prevailed and that was one.

You get a tremendous feeling of history and achievement when you are at Ibrox. The place has an aura about it. It was certainly a bit different to sitting in Jack Steedman's car looking at some used notes.

It didn't help either when I walked into the manager's office and came face to face with three of the biggest names in Rangers' history. I strolled in to be confronted by general manager Waddell, manager Wallace and assistant boss Willie Thornton. It was a formidable sight. And to be quite honest I felt a bit like a schoolboy up in front of the headmaster – only there were three of them. What I didn't feel like was a professional footballer who was in reasonable demand and who should have been holding all the aces in transfer talks.

Initially, Rangers offered me a signing-on fee of £5,000 but looking back I think even Messrs Waddell, Wallace and Thornton were a bit embarrassed by that because it didn't take much negotiating from me to get that figure doubled. The basic wage was around £150 and there were bonuses per point and I was happy enough because even before I signed I knew I would be joining Rangers regardless of the financial arrangements.

It was just about as good a bit of business as any club has ever done.

So it was farewell Clydebank, hello Rangers.

CHAPTER THREE

Born to be a Ranger

Ibrox, in those early days, was the perfect setting for a player like Cooper to display his wares.

Rangers were *the* team of the moment and although Davie's start was inauspicious to say the least – two defeats against Aberdeen and Hibs and a demonstration by disillusioned fans – it all sorted itself out eventually.

In October 1977 Coop's Rangers career began in earnest. Ironically, he kick-started it all against his former club with two goals in a 4–1 victory and things went from good to better.

'Gers strutted their stuff impressively in the League and only marginally less so in the League Cup although Forfar, of all clubs, did their best to put a huge dent in the Ibrox image by holding Coop and Co. to a 2–2 semi-final draw at the end of 90 minutes only to crumble in extra-time. But that was only a temporary hiccup in a sensational season when Rangers lifted the League Cup by beating Celtic 2–1, the championship and the Scottish Cup when a 2–1 win over Aberdeen completed a remarkable treble.

Coop's verdict on his own first season and contribution to the cause? 'Satisfactory but can do much better.'

As it turned out, that was easier said than done because Jock Wallace stunned the football world by walking out on Rangers and taking the manager's job at Leicester City. No one was more surprised or disappointed than Davie:

> The directors then hardly let Jock out of the door with his belongings before they took John Greig from the dressing-room and installed him in the big manager's office.
>
> Greigy didn't have far to go between the two but it might as well have been a million miles, such was the transformation between playing and captaining the side and becoming gaffer.
>
> It was a move that sparked even more controversy and from my point of view it did not prove a success. Jock had bought me and clearly rated me. John didn't appear to share that opinion quite as strongly and we didn't really hit it off when he went 'upstairs'.

Welcome to Ibrox from Tom Forsyth (left) and John Greig

Opposite: Proud to be a Ranger

I wasn't sure how he and I would get on as manager and player because I could foresee him having problems making the switch. I'm not knocking Greigy. I realise it couldn't have been easy for anyone to make a move like that and every manager has players he fancies more than others.

His time in charge at Ibrox was frustrating for me and when you consider he was there for more than five seasons you can maybe appreciate it wasn't the greatest time of my career.

Coop, indeed, was not flavour of the month and there is no doubt that in terms of skill and ability he had a few wasted seasons. There were times, to be fair, when he didn't help himself and he admitted as much when he declared: 'I unquestionably let myself go a bit. I had lost my way and was drifting aimlessly along.'

But you can only play if you're given the opportunity and on a number of occasions that was denied him because Greig felt others were better suited. He undoubtedly believed he had sound reasons for using Coop relatively

sparingly and he won both the Scottish Cup and the League Cup twice during his stint.

The hot seat, though, eventually became just too warm and when Wallace was reinstated for a second spell as boss after Alex Ferguson and Jim McLean both turned Rangers down no one was happier than Davie. 'He got me fit again by ordering me to lose five pounds in a month. I lost it in a week,' grinned the winger who knew not to cross the manager.

But Wallace went the way of all managers in due course and it has to be said that second time around he could never quite conjure up the old magic. If nothing else, though, he resurrected Davie's career even if Coop remained a big fish in a squad that was, by 'Gers standards, full of minnows.

But how that all changed when Graeme Souness was sensationally

A study in concentration

When the big-name players started to arrive at Ibrox there was
still no-one bigger than Coop. With Chris Woods . . . and Terry
Butcher . . . and together with fellow wingers, the legendary
Willie Waddell and Mark Walters

Davie and Maurice Johnston got along fine . . . in normal gear,
dressed up as Santa Claus or even with Ally McCoist!

appointed to follow Wallace! It was an amazing coup for Rangers and the dawn of a new era in every way, shape and form. Yet Davie, initially at least, viewed it all with some suspicion and even alarm. Jock Wallace, his long-time mentor, had gone and been replaced by a man Coop knew from his Scotland connections but most definitely not that well. And *no one* had any notion about Graeme Souness, manager of Rangers. As Coop later said with some honesty:

> I was pessimistic and concerned. I was concerned about myself because I wasn't sure what Graeme would do.
>
> I briefly believed he might want to bring in youngsters immediately and that would threaten my place at Ibrox. But I wasn't alone and I know every player had more or less the same feelings. In the end I reasoned, rightly or wrongly, that I had ability and why should a new manager want to do away with that.

The assessment was spot on. Souness knew quality when he saw it but if Coop was safe the same could not be said of others and large-scale changes quickly followed.

The lone big fish that was Coop was soon joined by some more very big fish!

Souness, as was his way, did nothing by halves and after an intriguing bid for Dundee United's Richard Gough was rejected the new boss turned his attentions to England and reversed the trend of players going south.

Colin West was first to arrive at Ibrox and he was quickly followed by the first of the genuinely massive deals when England keeper Chris Woods was enticed to come north. Miraculously, Terry Butcher was next and the world at large began to take notice of what was going on at Ibrox. Coop, for his part, was loving it all.

The football was loosely based on a mixture of Liverpool and Italian styles that had served Souness so well during his time. It was a passing game that suited Coop down to the ground. And once more his career was given a lift at a crucial moment.

Yet if a revolution – and that was what it was at Ibrox – is all about change the bottom line remains all about winning. 'Gers began that under Souness at the earliest opportunity – the Skol Cup final.

Ian Durrant and a penalty from Coop counted for Rangers while Brian

McClair's stunning strike was as much as Celtic got out of the occasion.

But it was an indication of the new standards around Ibrox that Souness didn't exactly go overboard about the success.

He made it clear it was simply a stepping-stone to greater things and just seconds after the final whistle he was reminding us, not for the first time, that the title was the priority.

There were a few hiccups along the way to that particular goal but in due course 'Gers grabbed their first title for nine years.

It goes almost without saying that it was a fantastic feeling, maybe even better than my first time which seemed like a century before.

It brought to an end a stunningly successful season for Rangers and I would hope I played my part in it all. Certainly, I enjoyed almost every minute of it and it made up in no small way for the years of nothing I had played through at Ibrox.

The season had not been without its disasters – Scottish Cup and Euro defeats against Hamilton and Borussia Moenchengladbach respectively – but the good far outweighed the bad and if there was a single reason for our success it was Souness.

He is a remarkable man and manager. He is also the first to pay tribute to Walter Smith. Wattie proved the ideal foil and although he simply can't play the game he knows a bit about it!

On the playing side everyone made a contribution but perhaps Terry Butcher stood out from the others. He's a man mountain and such a born winner that it's difficult to come to terms with the fact that he's English. Still, maybe he'll get over that.

Coop loved it all yet the enjoyment was tinged with a touch of frustration, as he confessed after that magnificent season:

I do feel a little bit frustrated that these good and exciting times at Ibrox have come a little too late for me. I can see success following success and I would have liked to be part of that for the years to come. But against that frustration is the realism that I have enjoyed a marvellous career that others would give their right arms for so I can't be greedy.

Souness, for his part, loved having Coop in his side. He declared then:

Any manager would be delighted to have a player of his ability, talent and skill. Basically, I believe he is more naturally gifted than Kenny Dalglish. And I'm delighted to say that from all accounts he has played better in recent times than he has done at any other stage of his career.

He has been a revelation and as far as I can tell the reason for his more consistent approach is simply that he is surrounded by better players.

From being a big fish in a small pool he is now just one of many outstanding players and it has taken a lot of pressure off him.

He is enjoying his football as a result and that is reflected in his performances which have been outstanding for me.

It was a glowing tribute from a consummate professional.

Opposite: Coop signs a new deal with Graeme Souness in close attendance

CHAPTER FOUR

Glory, Glory

Davie Cooper was good for Rangers – and Rangers were good for Davie Cooper. Club and player went together like salt and pepper.

Coop, of course, enjoyed good times at Motherwell and Clydebank where he started and finished a momentous career. But I don't think anyone at Fir Park or Kilbowie will be too upset if I say he was always truly synonymous with Rangers Football Club. And it's easy to see why.

Davie had 12 years at Ibrox. A dozen seasons that yielded tremendous honours. There were three League Championship medals, three Scottish Cup gongs and seven League Cup successes. On top of all that 20 of his 22 caps were won when he was playing for 'Gers. It is a phenomenal collection of prizes that deserves closer examination.

In his very first season at Ibrox following a £100,000 transfer from Clydebank the Ibrox side did the domestic treble. Yet it didn't exactly start out in style and the early weeks of the season didn't give any hint of the drama and excitement that was to follow.

Coop made his competitive debut for the Ibrox club on 13 August 1977 and 'Gers promptly lost 3–1 to Aberdeen at Pittodrie. A home defeat against Hibs followed and it was at Firhill on the third Saturday of the season that Davie first picked up a win bonus in the League. It was the catalyst for everything that was to follow.

Rangers began to play a bit and when they did Coop began to weigh in with a few goals. He got his first League goal in a six-goal draw against St Mirren at Love Street and then notched a double against his former Clydebank pals.

At the start of the second round of games, 'Gers beat Dons and Hibs to gain some revenge for their sticky early spell and, more importantly, they were top of the table. Even a 4–0 defeat at Pittodrie on Christmas Eve – Happy Christmas! – didn't prove anything other than a hiccup. And by the end of February 'Gers seemed to be cruising to the title after establishing a six-point lead over challengers Aberdeen.

Opposite: Just a few medals and trophies from the Coop collection

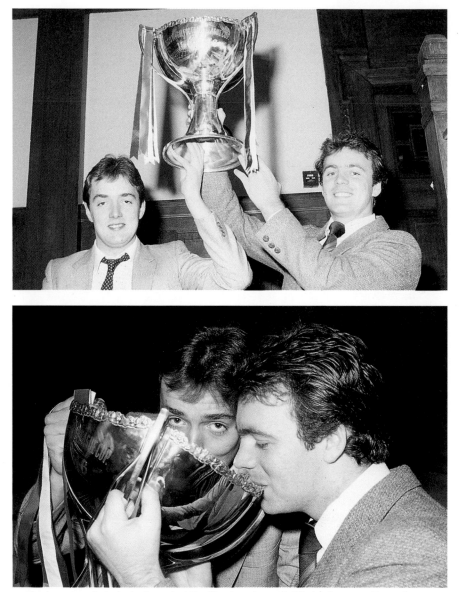

Davie gets a little help from Ian Redford as the pair lift the League Cup after an early 1980s' success against Dundee United. After all that heavy work, they needed a drink

But Dons promptly gave Rangers another severe drubbing – 3–0 at Ibrox – to put the Championship back into the melting pot and a late March defeat against Celtic further emphasised that the title was still up for grabs. It all became a bit fraught but Rangers stepped up a gear and won their last six games to land the big prize.

The League Cup went more or less according to plan with comfortable victories over St Johnstone, Aberdeen and Dunfermline and although there was a semi-final fright against lowly Forfar they continued their march and landed the trophy after a 2–1 victory over Celtic, with Coop a scorer.

It was a similar story in the Scottish Cup where Berwick, Stirling Albion, Kilmarnock and Dundee United all struggled and failed to stop the Ibrox mean machine.

Aberdeen in the final looked to present a more formidable obstacle bearing in mind the matches between the teams in the League but they too crashed as first Gordon Smith and then Bobby Russell took command. It was the finale of a glorious treble and Coop, incredibly, missed just one match throughout it all. He scored six League goals and one each in the other two tournaments.

The following season, after the shock departure of Jock Wallace and the appointment of John Greig as manager, 'Gers couldn't quite repeat their treble feat. But they still made it a double with successes in both cups.

Albion Rovers, Forfar, St Mirren and Arbroath fell by the wayside in the League Cup to set up an Old Firm semi-final that 'Gers eventually won in extra-time. And the Ibrox side almost had to go the same way in the final against Aberdeen but a last-gasp Colin Jackson winner in a 2–1 victory gave Greig his first trophy as boss.

In the Scottish Cup, Rangers hurdled Motherwell, Kilmarnock, Dundee and Partick Thistle en route to a Hampden final clash – or clashes as it turned out – with Hibs. It took three games to sort it all out and eventually it needed an own goal in extra time of the second replay to give Rangers the Cup.

Coop played in all those Scottish Cup ties but was in and out of the side in the League and League Cup. He still managed to score five Championship goals, three in the League Cup and two in the Scottish.

The next success was in 1981 when the Scottish Cup was again taken back to Ibrox. Airdrie were trounced in the opening round and St Johnstone beaten in a replay when a young Alistair McCoist scored the Saints' goal in a 3–1 scoreline.

Hibs and Morton were next to fall which left Dundee United standing between 'Gers and more glory. Coop was a substitute in the first game that ended 0–0 and was then recalled for the replay which he promptly turned into the Davie Cooper show by scoring the opener and setting up two more in a resounding 4–1 win.

Once more his appearances that season were limited in all competitions, and with just three in the League and that final goal in the Cup his strikes were rare as well.

So to 1982 and his 'lucky' tournament – the League Cup. The old-style section was won in some glory and included an 8–1 victory over Raith Rovers and the quarter-final against Brechin was also won in a canter. The semi against St Mirren was a lot more difficult but the Ibrox side edged through on a 4–3 aggregate and that put them in line for a final meeting with Dundee United. Once more Coop was instrumental in taking the trophy back to Ibrox as he notched a goal in 'Gers' 2–1 win. There were more appearances than in previous years for Davie and five goals in the three domestic competitions.

The tournament continued to be his happy hunting ground and in 1984 there was another spectacular triumph. By then, Jock Wallace had taken over the hot seat from John Greig and there is no doubt Coop's career picked up in tandem. He played 32 times in the League, nine in the League Cup and three in the Scottish Cup – plus substitute appearances – to signal he was back in business. And he scored nine goals into the bargain.

However, it was that League Cup that earned 'Gers their only triumph. Queen of the South were seen off with an 8–1 aggregate score and then the tournament moved into a section system with Rangers in alongside Hearts, Clydebank and St Mirren. Rangers' record read: played six, won six, drawn 0, lost 0, goals for 18, goals against 0. Pretty impressive stuff.

A 3–1 aggregate success over Dundee United in the semi-final set up a final clash with old rivals Celtic. It was an amazing Hampden battle as Celtic came back from 2–0 down to take the game to extra-time before Ally McCoist sealed victory in a thriller.

The next season was the same story all over again as 'Gers struggled in other tournaments yet kept their best for the League Cup campaign. By now it was the Skol Cup but it made no difference. Falkirk, Raith Rovers, Cowdenbeath and Meadowbank provided 'Gers with a gentle passage to the final but Dundee United were always going to be a bit different at Hampden.

In the end an Iain Ferguson goal after a move started by Coop settled the issue. But it was enough to keep that amazing record going in the competition and although 'Gers then missed a season they were soon back in business.

Graeme Souness had, in turn, succeeded Jock Wallace and sparked the Rangers revolution. He desperately wanted to mark his first season in charge by winning something – and it took him only a few months to deliver.

Coop was reborn yet again and surrounded as he was by better players as Souness stunned the football world by reversing the trend and getting top English players to travel north, he was back to his best.

Souness recognised that he had a genius on his hands – and Davie didn't disappoint him. He produced some electric performances although when you're talking electric there was almost a shock in the third round of the Skol Cup. Rangers had seen off Stenhousemuir comfortably enough when they were drawn to travel to Methil. East Fife then proceeded to make life extraordinarily difficult before 'Gers eased through 5–4 on penalties. Dundee and then Dundee United fell in a Tayside double until once more it was left to the Old Firm to contest the final. Ian Durrant and Coop from the penalty spot counted as Rangers won 2–1.

Davie played a large part in the march towards the club's first title since 1978 as well. Never more so than on the crucial day when Rangers travelled to Pittodrie on 2 May 1987. The Ibrox club had not won up north for five years – and they didn't win this time either. But as it turned out a 1–1 draw was enough as rivals Celtic went down 2–1 at home to Falkirk.

Coop steered a delightful cross onto the head of Terry Butcher and the big man did the rest. Brian Irvine managed an equaliser but with Celts losing it didn't matter too much. And how Coop, Souness and everyone else connected with Rangers enjoyed that success! But the new Ibrox boss was not one to rest on his laurels.

Almost as soon as the last ball of a tremendous season had been kicked he was consigning the double to the record books and planning ahead. Davie loved it all. He enjoyed sharing the midfield beat with his manager and he delighted in having genuine quality around him.

It was no surprise therefore when the next season – 1987–88 – brought

Following page: Davie with the trophy put up for his testimonial match against Bordeaux

yet more success to Ibrox. Coop had played 59 games in that double year – more than for some time – and he was in his element. But a Premier League and League Cup double was a hard act to follow.

Once more, though, Davie entered a new season like a fresh-faced youngster. He was bright, lively and enthusiastic. And he shared with Souness a burning ambition to secure more cups for the well-stocked Ibrox Trophy Room. They had to be content, though, with the Skol Cup once more as disaster struck in the Premier League and the Scottish Cup.

Even so, the Skol Cup provided enough drama and excitement for *all* the competitions. The run to the final was relatively uneventful. Stirling Albion, Dunfermline, Hearts and Motherwell were swatted aside to leave Aberdeen standing between Rangers and yet more glory. And what a final that turned out to be!

It was a glorious game punctuated by every conceivable kind of drama. But one moment stood above the rest for sheer theatre. And, naturally, it involved D. Cooper Esq. The free kick he struck past Jim Leighton is well-documented among the many tributes in this book and suffice to say few people have ever seen a ball hit harder. The keeper later joked with Coop that he nearly got to it and saved it. 'Yeah, on the way back out,' laughed Davie. It was, seriously, an awesome strike and it helped 'Gers to a 3–3 draw with the Ibrox side winning a dramatic penalty shoot-out.

That completed Davie's magnificent seven League Cup medals and although not everything went 'Gers' way that season his personal contribution over 50-odd matches was terrific. And it was no different the following year in what proved to be his last season at Ibrox.

The season started with his own testimonial match. Bordeaux was invited to Ibrox and over 43,000 turned out, not to see the French side but to honour one of Rangers' greatest-ever players. Coop was staggered. But it was just the beginning of another terrific season for the Souness-inspired side.

They won the League Cup again – without Coop – and romped away with the title courtesy of a 4–0 victory over Hearts at Ibrox on 29 April. Davie was not quite the influence he had been in previous years but he still

Previous page: Welcome to Motherwell from manager Tommy McLean, assistant Tom Forsyth and team-mate Bobby Russell who were all former Ibrox pals.

And wee Tam makes sure a jersey other than a blue one fits

played 22 League games in the 36-match campaign to prove he had a lot to offer even amidst the many and varied changes in personnel going on around him. Ibrox had a revolving door then as now and players came and went on a regular basis.

Coop, meanwhile, had enjoyed some of the best months of his career under the leadership of Souness, but his reign at Ibrox was nearly over.

Through that summer he kept himself fit as ever by lapping Strathclyde Park but he knew better than anyone that he wasn't getting any younger and that he might struggle to maintain a regular first-team place at ever-changing Ibrox. Souness knew that too so when, in August, Motherwell made an audacious bid to snatch the local boy they weren't discouraged. The then Fir Park manager, Tommy McLean, always maintained it was the best £50,000 he ever spent and who could possibly argue with that?

Coop left Rangers simply because he wanted to play. He loved Ibrox and everything about the club but couldn't handle sitting on the sidelines when he felt – rightly – he still had a lot to offer. Rangers' loss was Motherwell's gain.

Against all the odds, he collected more silverware. First and foremost he put Motherwell Football Club on the map. He gave the Fir Park outfit a credibility that they maybe lacked and was an instant hero to the fans who recognised – as so many had before them – genuine skill and ability. And, incredibly, he helped them to their first trophy in years.

Not even Davie suspected he could be the difference between relative mediocrity and a cup-winning side. But there's no doubt much of 'Well's new-found success was down to him. Motherwell's famous triumph is documented elsewhere in this book and it was a fitting tribute to Davie's contribution.

Latterly at Fir Park he was also doing some coaching with the young players and he enjoyed the involvement. But, as ever, Davie wanted to play more than anything. So in December 1993 he was allowed to depart Fir Park on the back of generous thanks for all he had done for the club. And maybe it should be no surprise that it was Jack Steedman who gave him the opportunity to keep on performing. It's really quite appropriate that the man who gave him his start should also have given him his final chance to continue doing what he did best.

GORDON SMITH

I'd never really seen Coop play before we joined Rangers at around the same time. When I did, I couldn't believe just how good he was.

Very few Scottish players have possessed that kind of skill and ability and it was a pleasure to play alongside him.

When I later moved to the continent to pursue my career I saw lots of fine players with marvellous talent. But none was better than Davie.

PETER McCLOY

He became interested in the coaching side of things quite late on and was always going to have a future in the game. He had so much to offer younger players.

46

Hat's the game. Davie and Sandy Jardine make like Coop.
Tommy Cooper that is

SANDY JARDINE

When Davie joined Rangers a lot of us were nearing the end of our careers. He came as a shy, quiet young lad. He went on to develop but was never flamboyant or loud and was, basically, just a nice person.

Like Jim Baxter, whom I also played alongside, he had the kind of rare talent you couldn't coach into people. His goal in the Drybrough Cup against Celtic was one in a lifetime and it overshadowed me because I scored one of my best goals that day and it hardly got a mention.

BOBBY RUSSELL

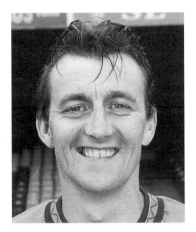

I was Davie's room-mate for ten years when we were at Ibrox together so I think I knew him as well as most. He was a fantastic player and a lovely man.

I have so many memories of him that it's difficult to pick out just a few. One of his greatest moments on the park, though, was in the Drybrough Cup final in 1979. Davie picked up a pass from Alex MacDonald, flicked the ball up and over Roddie MacDonald, beat Murdo MacLeod and Tom McAdam and then did to Alan Sneddon what he had done to big Roddie. After all that he proceeded to fire a great drive past Peter Latchford! It was as good a goal as anyone could wish to see – never mind score – and that game will always be remembered because of that special moment. Yet, ironically, Sandy Jardine also scored probably the best goal of his career that day and John MacDonald also notched his first-ever goal for Rangers. Both were totally forgotten because of Coop's effort.

I remember, too, a Scottish Cup final against Dundee United in 1981. Davie hadn't played in the first game which ended 0–0 after extra time but he was recalled for the replay and promptly ran the entire show. The rest of us were bit players that night. Coop was magnificent. He scored the opening goal and then helped me to one and John MacDonald to a couple while Davie Dodds got United's consolation. I don't know if he was trying to prove a point after not playing first time round but if that was the case he certainly did it!

He was, though, just such a good player. And certainly he was as good as I ever played alongside. We had a great understanding and as long as you were prepared to make the runs at the right time and into the right space you knew Coop would get the ball to you.

That partnership we had at Rangers was special and I was delighted when we were able to continue it at Motherwell. He helped me enormously but there again lads at Fir Park like Rab McKinnon and former 'Well stars like Phil O'Donnell and Tam Boyd will tell you the same.

Mind you, it was different off the park because there's no doubt he abused my hospitality when we roomed together! He was a nightmare! Basically, I was his tea-boy. I would make the tea one minute and then next time round suggest it might be his turn. He would never bother, though, and just let me get on with it again. I would hurl insults at him and tell him I had made him a player and so on but it never moved him to put the kettle on!

On a slightly different subject, I recall the two of us going into a bar in Eindhoven in Holland. We were only going in for a quick beer – but we didn't realise how quick. We were only in the place seconds when we thought there was something odd about it. We were right. It turned out to be a gay bar and as soon as we realised there was something fishy about it we were off. I actually think that was as fast as I ever saw him move.

His death affected me badly because he and I had been doing some promotional work up north and he was the last person in the world I ever worried about from a health point of view. It's just so tragic because he had such a great future in front of him as well as such a glorious past.

DEREK JOHNSTONE

The biggest tribute that can be paid to Davie was the astonishing scenes after he so tragically died. The measure of the man was shown then.

Fans from all over the world, from every different club and from all walks of life united in grief. It was a mark of respect for Coop. It showed what a great footballer he was and also proved what a nice man he was into the bargain. He would never have believed it because he never got carried away with his own ability.

Davie would have been staggered that Celtic supporters – and fans from all those other clubs – respected him *that* much. And he would have been a little bit embarrassed as well. Davie was so easy-going that all those tributes would have made him blush.

He knew he was a good player but that never made him big-headed in any way, shape or form. He always had time for people, he was always willing to help and I can't imagine he ever really changed from when he was a youngster. And money was never important to him. If it had been all about cash he would have moved from Rangers to another club and picked up thousands of pounds. But he just wanted to play for the Ibrox club like he did for Clydebank and Motherwell. Money genuinely never entered his head. As long as he had a few quid for his bets on the horses and for a beer or two he was happy.

From a playing point of view there is no doubt in my mind that he was one of Europe's greatest players. He could even have been one of the world's best if he had left these shores and gone continental because I think he might have improved even more with a top side in Italy. But he wasn't half a good player anyway.

He was to Rangers a bit like what Brian Laudrup has been in that he did something special in *every* game he played. He could have been a Brazilian!

There are so many outstanding memories of his playing career that it's difficult to pick out just a few. But one thing's for sure, he made my job a whole lot easier when we played together. I'm the first to admit I couldn't have done what I did without someone like him. He, together with Tommy McLean, supplied the ammunition for me and made my job much more straightforward. I don't know the percentage of goals he set up for me but there were dozens. And, strangely, Coop got as much pleasure out of those 'assists' as he did from scoring himself. When he did notch they were never just simple tap-ins. He was like Mark Hughes of Wales in that respect – his goals were always spectacular. The one that sticks out in my mind particularly has to be the strike in the Drybrough Cup final against Celtic. It was probably the greatest goal I have ever seen. It eclipsed great efforts by Sandy Jardine and John MacDonald and was, quite simply, remarkable.

There was another not bad effort in a League Cup final, also against Celtic, in the late 1970s when I jumped higher than I've ever done in my life to get out of the way of his shot. I realised when the ball broke to Coop that I was going to block his effort so I jumped and claimed an assist of my own when his strike nearly burst the net!

But, as I say, he derived just as much fun from setting others up and there was an amazing reverse pass to Ian Durrant that let the wee man in for a cup final goal that I remember.

That was Coop at his best. And his best was quite amazing.

JIMMY NICHOLL

Jimmy Nicholl's glorious career took him around the world. It brought him medals and memories, trophies and tributes, cups and Northern Ireland caps. It allowed him to view from near and far the world's greatest players. 'And my lasting memory of Davie Cooper is that he was one of the best players I have ever seen,' admitted the Ulsterman.

Coop and Nick were great friends but don't for a second be fooled into thinking that clouded any judgements. Nicholl is too shrewd for that. He himself was an outstanding player and has since gone on to enjoy a quite remarkable career as a manager so he knows a thing or two about football.

He also knows a thing or two about people in general, and he had enormous respect for Davie both as a player and a person.

I can't remember Coop ever believing himself to be something special, and that in itself was remarkable because so many players – and indeed so many people – have delusions of grandeur. That was simply not the case with Davie because he was, basically, just an ordinary guy.

He had no airs and graces, no big ideas about himself, no belief that he was in any way better than anyone else, and that was proved time and again. After all, how many top-class footballers can be seen getting on and off public transport regularly! Coop did that all the time.

He was terribly modest and in many ways he was embarrassed by his fame. The only times I saw him being different to that was in five-a-side knockabout games when he never tired of telling team-mates and opposition players alike how good he was! But he was only doing it for a laugh or to wind people up.

He never seriously meant it although, heaven knows, he was entitled to shout it from the rooftops because he *was* an enormously gifted footballer. But great players never have to tell you how good they are and that was the situation with Coop.

Others could see for themselves in an instant that he was extraordinary. He really could have played anywhere in the world and not looked in any way out of place.

And Coop's brilliance gave Nick many a moment of pleasure when the pair were team-mates – and close pals – at Rangers.

There was that astonishing dribble against Ilves Tampere; the remarkable Drybrough Cup goal against Celtic that was an astonishing display of brilliance. But for me the most magical moment was that incredible free kick against Aberdeen in the Skol Cup final.

Mind you, if Nick had had his way that fantastic effort might never have found its way into the record books and annals of football fame.

I dabbled with the idea of taking it myself, I had visions of being able to curl it into the corner past Aberdeen keeper Jim Leighton. But maybe it's just as well I didn't try! Coop, instead, took the bull by the horns and blasted in that amazing strike.

It was hit with awesome power and I don't think in all my travels I have seen a ball hit harder. The ball was in and out of the net again almost before poor Jim moved a muscle. It really was a stunning goal by any standards.

But if the power of that effort remains a vivid memory for Jimmy there are other, far less spectacular, touches from Coop that he recalls with as much pleasure.

His little touches were just as clever. I loved the way he could thread the ball through the smallest gap in a defence or the way he could deliver a pass to perfection. They were just as impressive qualities as Davie's ability to hit the ball hard. Altogether, they made him a very special player.

Others, I'm sure, would acknowledge the debt they owe him. He 'made' guys like Derek Johnstone and Ally McCoist, for instance, and later at Motherwell others like Phil O'Donnell and Rob McKinnon.

What I liked most about Davie is that he left his mark on and off the pitch.

STUART MUNRO

Davie could have made a fortune by moving down south but he resisted the temptation because he was a Rangers man through and through.

I have never seen anyone to touch him. Ryan Giggs is good but Davie was the best I've ever seen. And I'm sure if he had gone to England or even abroad he would have been an even bigger name but he was happy at Ibrox. When Graeme Souness went to Ibrox he began to enjoy himself even more because he was in the company of better players. If he had been just coming to his peak then and had been, say, 25, then I'm sure Graeme would have built his revolution around Davie. He could have been even better which is frightening.

They say once a Ranger, always a Ranger, and that's fitting for Coop.

GRAEME SOUNESS

I always believed that Davie Cooper was a more naturally gifted player than even the great Kenny Dalglish. And that is high praise.

Furthermore, I always reckoned that any manager in the world would have been delighted to have a player of Coop's ability, talent and skill in his team. I recall saying the same things in the foreword to Davie's autobiography *True Blue*. Then, I was delighted to take the opportunity to recount the tale of his nickname 'Albert' which stemmed from the Coronation Street character Albert Tatlock who was always moaning. I could always tell if Coop was going to have a good game if he came into Ibrox and was moaning even more than usual!

Around that time I'm delighted to say he played better than at any other stage in his career. He was a revelation and it was simply because he was surrounded by better players. Guys like Terry Butcher and Chris Woods were top-class professionals and Davie responded accordingly.

From being a big fish in a small pond he became just one of many outstanding players and it took a lot of pressure off him. He began enjoying his football again as a result and it was reflected in some outstanding performances for me when I was manager of Rangers.

I played alongside Davie for Scotland on several occasions so I knew what I was getting. He was tremendously consistent at that time and was a considerable influence on the side.

It was a pleasure to have worked with him and to have known him.

WALTER SMITH

Davie Cooper had so much skill and ability he could have played for any team in the world. I genuinely believe that to be the case. Yet the funny thing was, he was never interested in trying his luck anywhere else. He only ever wanted to play in Scotland and, for most of his career, for Rangers.

He was always a tremendous player for this club but when Graeme Souness and I moved into Ibrox he was transformed. There is no doubt in my mind that was because he was surrounded by better players. For a long time Coop was the outstanding player at Ibrox but when big names like Terry Butcher and Chris Woods joined the club he wasn't on his own up there any longer. That took a bit of pressure off him and he responded brilliantly.

I believe that the first couple of seasons we had here Davie played the best football of his career, and that is saying something. He was magnificent and most important of all he was magnificent consistently. His performances were terrific week in, week out. He was unquestionably as good a player as I've seen. He was a special talent.

Helping Walter Smith launch a new 'Gers video

It's actually impossible to come to any conclusion about how much he would have been worth in the transfer market. But the fact that he made so many goals for others and scored his fair share made him a very valuable player to Rangers. Equally, I'm sure Clydebank and Motherwell would say the same thing. He gave those clubs tremendous service as well in a wonderful career. You simply don't get players of that quality coming along very often.

But he couldn't half moan! Davie's pet hates were referees and coaches which meant I got my fair share of stick because I refereed some training games and also did a lot of the coaching!

I got earache but it was worth it to be able to marvel at a very special talent.

TOMMY McLEAN

A chance remark over dinner led to Motherwell completing the best bit of transfer business the club had ever done or is ever likely to do. Then Fir Park manager Tommy McLean was out for a bite to eat with Ricky Jordan, a pal of Davie Cooper's, and the two were chatting about football in general.

Ricky casually admitted that he felt Davie might soon be ready for a change. He knew Coop loved Rangers but he also realised that because he wasn't getting a regular game at Ibrox he was becoming a little frustrated. After all, the only thing Coop wanted to do was play. And when he wasn't playing he could get, well, a bit crochety! It was enough to sow a seed in McLean's mind although almost as quickly as it entered his head he dismissed it again.

I didn't really think Coop would entertain signing for Motherwell, but I was interested enough to pursue the thought eventually. I asked Ricky if Coop would be even remotely interested and when the player's close pal said he thought he would it was enough to spur me into some serious action.

I spoke first to Rangers' assistant boss Walter Smith and then manager

Above: Coop always liked a goal and so did his 'Well team-mates

Right: Rain, hail or shine . . . Davie stood out

Opposite: Majestic was the only word for all this style

Graeme Souness and they were brilliant. They could have made life a bit difficult and asked for an enormous fee but Rangers deserve tremendous credit for the way they handled it all.

Basically, they wanted to do Davie a favour in view of his tremendous service to the club so we agreed a fee of just £50,000 and I spoke to Davie about the possibilities. I was delighted with his response. He was very enthusiastic about the prospect although, to be fair, he was a bit unhappy at the thought of leaving Ibrox. But he knew he was getting to the stage where with all the new players going to Ibrox he simply wasn't guaranteeed his place so it didn't take him long to agree to go to Fir Park.

It must be the best money Motherwell ever spent because he lifted the club to another level. We had gone through the workmanlike stage when, to be honest, we had to fight and bite and scratch for every result we got.

Davie and Tom Boyd all smiles after a goal against Dundee

We needed to take things a step further and the signing of Davie did that.

Many people, though, thought Coop was going out to grass when he left Rangers for Motherwell but wee Tam knew differently.

It was never a gamble. I suppose there might have been an element of concern from some people over his age but it was never a worry to me.

If you have the kind of quality Coop had then age really doesn't come into it. As long as a player getting on a little bit has kept his enthusiasm there is no problem – and Davie was certainly enthusiastic. He also had too much pride to just let his career drift at that stage. He really wanted to do well for Motherwell and, of course, he did.

Coop, in fact, exceeded all Fir Park expectations as he gave the club a new credibility. He produced all his old magic as his career was kick-started once more.

Although some ex-Rangers players find it difficult to be accepted at other clubs when they move on the Fir Park fans recognised they had been handed a jewel.

They took to Davie right away because they knew of his ability and also because they could see he was so keen to perform for the club. They also recognised, as did everyone else at Fir Park, what a big influence Davie was on everything around him.

McLean, of course, had known Cooper from their Rangers days so he knew better than most just what he had got.

He was a lot more outgoing when he went to Motherwell than he was when I first knew him at Ibrox. But all through his career he could spot hangers-on and people he didn't fancy a lot. He could see through the chancers that are around football.

The overriding thing about Davie Cooper was his skill, talent and ability. He still had plenty of that going for him when he went to Fir Park. He produced some memorable performances for Motherwell and he was always extra keen to do well against Celtic for instance.

Coop loved playing against the Parkhead side and he knew that although

Right: Arm in arm with Hibs defender Willie Miller

Below: Someone's out of step . . . and it was more likely to be Aberdeen's David Winnie

Opposite: Davie and Airdrie's Jimmy Sandison make it a case of 'never mind the ball, get on with the game'

Even the polis can't help but admire

their fans would give him a hard time it was because they recognised the damage he could inflict on Celtic. It was a kind of respect. When he was at Rangers and then at Motherwell he would always love games against the Parkhead side, and invariably he would play extremely well.

I well remember big Roy Aitken trying to kick him up and down the park once but all Coop did was dance clear and continue to set up mayhem. Falkirk, for reasons I never did discover, was another of the teams he was always keen to do well against. He produced a superb performance against them in Motherwell's run to the Scottish Cup final in 1991.

That success, of course, was down in no small way to Davie. He had helped put so much belief into the players and they gained confidence from playing alongside a player who had seen and done it all before.

He was always passing on his experience to younger lads and even now players like Rab McKinnon and Tom Boyd will tell you how much they owe to Davie.

I suppose that Cup run was the highlight of Coop's time at Fir Park and it was certainly the spell when he and the club got tremendous publicity.

Gary McGinnis of St Johnstone tries, and fails, to stop Coop in his tracks

Above: Coop tries one for size against his old team as Richard Gough and Gary Stevens watch anxiously

Left: Stevie Crawford, a star of the new generation, watches and learns

Turning on the style indoors as well with Ian Angus and
Celtic's Mike Galloway trailing

But all the time he was doing so much more for Motherwell. He was
great to have about the place and he was very good on the P.R. side of things
because he had learned how to handle that side of football. He was some
signing.

*Motherwell reaped the benefit in that extraordinary Scottish Cup run especially.
They sounded the first warning of intent as early as the third round back in
January.*

*'Well travelled to meet Aberdeen at Pittodrie and a game against the
holders was expected to bring the Fir Park club's Cup involvement to a sticky
end almost before it had begun. But a Steve Kirk goal was enough to snatch*

Above: Davie enjoyed Old Firm battles . . . here he was all power and precision as Celtic prepared to count the cost

Right: Standing still at Fir Park for a second

Top: This time he's causing Ray Wilkins, among others, some problems in a 'Well v 'Gers clash

Bottom: When you've played alongside a genius, you know it takes two to even attempt to stop him. This time the unhappy task fell most immediately to Gary Stevens

With the Cup and a sponsored car. And that after years of never bothering to learn to drive!

Opposite: It's a piece of cake . . . and a birthday surprise from brewers Tennents

a dramatic victory and start the long haul towards Hampden in some style.

That tie against Falkirk at Fir Park provided some fourth round magic and a Nick Cusack double, plus a goal each from Joe McLeod and Kirk again saw off the Bairns despite efforts from Sammy McGivern and Alex Taylor.

The quarter-finals, though, produced a bit of a hiccup to Coop and Company. A 0–0 home draw with Morton didn't exactly reinforce the view that it was to be 'Well's year. And neither did a 1–1 replay result when Boyd and John Gahagan scored the goals.

That opened the door to a penalty shoot-out and the inevitable prospect of

Above: Ouch! Davie gets a dull one from Dunfermline's Mark Bowes

Opposite: Maybe not at his most elegant but almost certainly still effective

Perfect balance, perfect poise . . . just perfect

Previous pages: Coop's concentration doesn't waver and surprise, surprise the ball is attached to his *left* foot

Congrats, pal. Davie and Iain Ferguson give it the hands-on approach

Opposite: Davie congratulates Fir Park team-mate Dougie Arnott on another goal

some poor player becoming the fall guy. On that occasion it was Morton's Mark Pickering who was singled out by fate and 'Well scraped their way through to the semi-finals 5–4 on spot kicks.

No one could accuse the Fir Park side of doing it the easy way and that was confirmed again in the semis against Celtic. The two teams drew 0–0 at Hampden at the first attempt and then promptly made up for that no-score bore with a six-goal replay thriller.

Some of the goals were good, some were great and a couple were absolutely spectacular. Celtic's efforts were rewarded by a Boyd own goal and another from

Above: 'Now then, who will I fool next?' could be the thought for the moment

Opposite: In action against Hair-drie!

Above: Smile please . . . with 'Well team-mate Ian Angus

Opposite: Davie lifts the Scottish Cup aloft in a moment of undiluted triumph after Motherwell's thrilling final victory over Dundee United

Above: Outside Fir Park and raring to go

Opposite: High flying Coop with Colin O'Neill watching

Anton Rogan while Motherwell counted through a Dougie Arnott double.

From being 2–1 down, 'Well moved into overdrive and scored two goals that have seldom been bettered at the national stadium. Colin O'Neill's stunning 35-yard drive flew past Pat Bonner into the top corner like an Exocet missile – and it caused Celtic's Cup hopes just as much damage.

The wee Irishman, sadly forced out of football prematurely through injury, has the memory of that strike to warm him through long winter nights.

And when Stevie Kirk – who else – curled in a magnificent fourth Motherwell were home and dry and looking forward to a final clash with Dundee United. It was billed as the Battle of the Brothers – Jim McLean v Tommy – but it was another extraordinary chance for one D. Cooper to add to his illustrious career *record. And the bold Coop did just that in the most entertaining Scottish Cup final for decades.*

It was a remarkable spectacle. A roller-coaster of a game. And certainly a feast of football for the 57,319 crowd. Coop, naturally, was to the fore.

Iain Ferguson and Dave Bowman scored to get the ball well and truly rolling and then Motherwell swept into a 3–1 lead courtesy of Phil O'Donnell – set up by Davie – and Ian Angus.

Back came United with goals from John O'Neil and Darren Jackson to tie it up once more and take an amazing final into extra time. Then Coop took another hand in proceedings, swung over a corner and there was that man Kirk to notch what proved to be the winner.

Coop eventually went off to tumultuous applause and to let O'Neill have a few precious minutes of the action but it was another tremendous feat from the winger.

After that Cup final and after a remarkable 1992–93 season when he played in every one of Motherwell's Premier League matches he was getting more and more into coaching. As Tam explained:

I got Davie started with the youngsters and the 'S' form lads. He enjoyed it and was doing well but even then he wanted to play more than anything so when Clydebank came in for him we knew he would have a better chance of playing regularly and let him go.

But he remains the outstanding signing of them all.

Opposite: Sitting comfortably in a 'Well strip

CHAPTER FIVE

Coop and Scotland

Davie never tried to fool anyone over his often controversial views on Scotland and Scottish football. He was, as ever, straightforward and direct and he knew full well that not everyone would like what they read or heard. But in much the same way that he waltzed past despairing defenders so he left administrators trailing in his wake.

Coop wasn't interested in currying favour – even if his views were hot stuff! He would rather tell it the way it was and his message for those who didn't like it was short and sweet. Too bad. In many ways that applied most to our international set-up.

Davie was always of the opinion that it was a club that paid your wages and therefore it was the club who had first call on your services. They were the bread and butter – Scotland was the jam.

Playing for Scotland has never been a matter of life and death for me since I first represented my country at amateur level all those years ago. I know that sounds bad and I appreciate that most kids, and for that matter any amount of adults, would give their right arms to wear the dark blue jersey. I understand that.

Don't get me wrong – I was honoured when I was chosen but if it was ever a case of club against country then I believe I was duty-bound to go for the people who pay my wages week in, week out. It's just the way I am and while other players might expect and anticipate representative honours I never consider the possibility. If it happens great. If it doesn't, well, there's no point in losing sleep over the matter.

Maybe that smacked a little of a lack of enthusiasm to some people and if it did it would go a long way to explaining why a man of almost unrivalled ability won just 22 caps with Rangers and Motherwell.

Opposite: Compulsory reading . . . the *Sporting Life*. And Coop gets into training for race day

That is a paltry total when you look at some of the players who have won many more for Scotland over the years. It's almost a national disgrace, in fact. But Coop never complained and maybe he knew deep down that his attitude had hindered his progress at international level. Yet, when he played, he enjoyed it and he had many fond – and interesting – memories.

He started out in the Under-18s but it was really in the Under-21s that he began to catch the eye. And he was in decent company. His team-mates in those early international days included names like Roy Aitken, Willie Miller, Dave Narey, Frank McGarvey and George Burley. And, even then, boss Andy Roxburgh was a stickler for detail:

> Sometimes when you're away with squads time can lie a bit heavily on your hands but Andy to his credit ensured that never happened. In fact, he would make sure every minute of the day was accounted for and that was no bad thing. He worked on the theory that we should all stick together as much as possible so that the better we knew each other off the park the better we would get on together on the park. It made sure there were no cliques and he put a lot of time and effort into ensuring everything was just right. His attention to detail was unbelievable but it helped make us feel important and we had some good results on the strength of it.

But after that sortie into the international arena Coop then drifted out of it just as quickly as he spent every waking minute trying to establish himself at Ibrox.

So it was 1979 before he picked up his first cap even if his initial experiences of the senior squad had come two years earlier. Coop was named in the Scotland squad before he had actually kicked a ball for Rangers.

Ally MacLeod included him for a fact-finding trip to Chile, Argentina and Brazil which was designed to give the players and officials a taste of what to expect at the following year's World Cup.

The squad, including a young Coop, bristled with big names: Kenny Dalglish, Martin Buchan, Bruce Rioch, Danny McGrain, Lou Macari and Willie Johnston were all aboard.

Home-loving Coop took next to no time to discover what international travelling is all about:

> When we got to the hotel in Santiago I discovered my one and only suitcase

was missing. I couldn't believe it. There I was on my first senior trip with Scotland and all I had to wear were the clothes I stood up in. It's just as well my new club boss Jock Wallace was 10,000 miles away because he was a stickler for smartness and I looked more like Worzel Gummidge than Beau Brummel.

The rest of the lads were great and helped me out with bits and pieces but I have to admit Gordon McQueen's shirt was like a coat on me.

And Coop's problems didn't end there.

It's safe to say his Scotland career didn't exactly get off to a flyer because no sooner was the clothes problem sorted than Davie was getting into bother, along with room-mate Jim Stewart, with boss MacLeod.

It was a minor incident but it always narked Coop and as he admitted himself: 'It made me wonder about Ally'. The problem arose when the players were told to report downstairs in their hotel for 7 p.m. Cooper and Stewart duly made it out of the lift with ten minutes to spare but were greeted by MacLeod demanding to know where they had been and did they realise the time. Davie never quite understood what all that fuss was about but it didn't do much to instil in him confidence in the management.

As it turned out he didn't play on the trip although, as an untried youngster, he was never over-confident he would see any action. But it was a long way to take a player just to sit on the bench and maybe Ally's bizarre behaviour over the duo's timing soured him a bit.

Yet Coop basically enjoyed the experience nevertheless. Well, most of it. The wee boy from Hamilton had his eyes opened on that tour.

After we won 4–2 in Chile it was on to Argentina and everyone was a bit taken aback when we saw the 'plane which was to transport us over the mountains to Buenos Aires. It was painted a strange shade of pink and although no one thought any more about it we were a bit upset when we landed and were told it was that colour because it showed up well against the mountain snow!

And the journey into our hotel from the airport was unbelievable. The local police were obviously rehearsing for the World Cup because we had a couple of out-riders escorting us and they didn't mess about. The guys on the bikes would go up alongside cars who were going too slowly – maybe they were only doing 70 mph through the city centre! – and rather than mess about with a lecture they literally kicked the sides of the vehicles as they went along. Later on, we even got to the stage of exchanging badges for bullets with the local cops.

Maybe Coop and the rest of the Scotland stars should have stuck to that because the Argentinian national side of the time was notorious.

England's Trevor Cherry had been sent off in ridiculous circumstances not long before and poor Willie Johnston, who was kicked from one end of the park to another, was eventually moved to describe his 'marker' as a 'Sumo wrestler in studs'.

Coop had an anxious moment of his own when Willie stayed down after one particularly nasty challenge. MacLeod ordered Davie to warm-up and Coop remembered the moment. 'I don't think Ally realised it was raining coins. It really was very hostile and I wasn't too upset when Willie picked himself up and carried on.'

So Coop never made it then and he didn't get on against Brazil in the last game either. But a cap call proper wasn't that far away.

It was September, 1979, when his international career was kick-started. By then Jock Stein had replaced MacLeod and the legendary manager called Davie in for a friendly against Peru. Coop did all right in a 1–1 draw even if he was eventually substituted by John Wark and just a month later he was back in the Scotland squad – albeit on the bench – for a vital European Championship match against Austria.

This time it was his turn to go on – for Arthur Graham – and once more the game ended 1–1. But that was that for Coop for a long time and his absence coincided with his struggling years at Ibrox.

When Jock Wallace replaced John Greig at Rangers Coop's career went back on track at international level. And there were more memorable moments. None more so than the triumphant, and at the same time tragic, night in Cardiff when Scotland drew with Wales to make it through to the 1986 World Cup finals.

During the qualifying games, the Scots produced some outstanding results with a 3–1 victory over Spain as Davie recalled:

> It was the best performance at that level I have been involved in. Everything fell into place and with Jim Bett behind me I believe it was one of my own best performances as well.
>
> Every one of us was at the top of his form and it really was a privilege to be in the side. We won 3–1 with Mo Johnston getting two and Kenny Dalglish the other in a style only he can.

That was one of the results that set up a nerve-tingling decider on 10 September 1985 between Scotland and Wales in Cardiff.

Jock Stein named me for a place on the bench and I felt that if things were going against us I might get a chance. But obviously I was hoping I wouldn't be needed because that would mean Scotland, who only needed a point, would have everything under control. And we were confident that would be the case. Wales were a good, competent side and they had two tremendous strikers in Ian Rush and Mark Hughes. We were well aware they would be the main dangers to our ambitions and when Hughes scored the opening goal it might have had them singing in the Welsh valleys but it struck the wrong chord with us.

All of a sudden Mexico and the World Cup seemed like a distant dream and it wasn't a pleasant feeling after all we had been through. That was how it stood at half-time and Mr Stein looked tense when he talked to us at the interval although managers always tend to be like that.

There was some unexpected drama then when Jim Leighton informed the manager he was having trouble with one of his contact lenses. That came as a bit of a shock to everyone, including his club manager Alex Ferguson who was Jock's assistant, because up till then no one knew he wore the things!

Alan Rough was hastily stripped for action and Jock also singled me out to say I might be pushed on if the scoreline didn't change.

My chance came midway through the second half when Jock told Fergie to get me out for a warm-up. After a couple of runs I was summoned back and told to get ready. Then Jock said to me: 'Go out and play wide on the left. Go at them and try and get behind them as often as possible.' I didn't consider for a second that those few words would be the last order he would give.

I went on for Gordon Strachan and early on I nutmegged Joey Jones just to boost my confidence!

Then with ten minutes left and with Mexico fading even further into the distance Scotland were awarded a penalty. There is no doubt in my mind that it was a legitimate award. I knew straight away that the job would fall to me. Wee Strach and I were the nominated penalty takers but since I had replaced him it narrowed the choice.

Just in case there were any lingering doubts in my mind big Roy Aitken walked over with the ball in his hands and told me to get on with it. I just wish I had a pound for every time someone has asked me since how I felt at that moment. It's not easy but I have to say I wasn't especially nervous despite the bedlam with the Scots fans going wild with delight and the Welsh supporters simply going wild. My initial thought was simply that there we were, just a few minutes from making an inglorious exit from the World Cup and I had a chance to salvage it all. It was only much later that it really hit me and I started shaking!

What would have happened if I had missed it? Imagine being labelled forever with the tag of the man who cost Scotland the chance to go to Mexico.

But my problem, apart from trying to keep cool, was deciding where I would place the spot kick. I recalled in a flash the previous time I had lined up a penalty against keeper Neville Southall and I nearly blew a fuse as I tried to settle on whether or not I should stick to my usual habit of placing it to the keeper's right. Then I remembered Southall had nearly saved my last one against him so I opted to change. This all happened in a few seconds although it could have been an hour as far as I was concerned.

Eventually I stepped up, hit it well and watched in horror as Neville dived the correct way and looked for all the world as if he was going to save it. But after what seemed an eternity the ball somehow squirmed over the line. Big Roy hit me first and then the rest piled in and when I looked over to the bench Alex Ferguson and a few others were also celebrating.

I never thought too much of it at the time because he never showed much elation, or for that matter disappointment, but Jock Stein stayed in his seat. Maybe that was significant.

It probably was. Coop's successful spot kick sent the whole of Scotland into raptures and the whole of Wales into woe.

But very soon after the two nations – and the rest of the football world – forgot the penalty, the result and the World Cup. Coop takes up the story once more.

The players all started congratulating each other after the final whistle, fans came onto the pitch, television cameras and radio microphones were thrust into our faces.

But then, as I neared the dug-out, I came face-to-face with Fergie who said: 'Big Jock has collapsed. We don't know what's wrong. Stay there for a minute.'

I turned to tell the others to wait and eventually we made our way to the dressing-room where Alex once more said that Jock had collapsed.

No one else said anything and there was an eery quiet which was only broken when Scottish Football Association president David Will came in and said: 'We've lost the manager. Jock's passed away.'

It was a dreadful moment when nothing, least of all a football match, seemed to have any significance. No one moved, no one did anything.

In due course we sorted ourselves out into some kind of order and made our way out of the stadium to the team bus where groups of fans stood around obviously only too well aware of the tragedy.

The worst moment, and there were many bad ones, came when the coach pulled away from the stadium and I asked myself what we were doing leaving when the gaffer was still there.

Later, much later that night, I thought back to the evening and briefly considered that I had just scored the most important goal of my career yet it meant nothing really.

Football was put firmly into perspective and I think a great many people reflected then that maybe it didn't matter so much after all.

Maurice Johnston congratulates Davie after his penalty against Wales in Cardiff edged Scotland closer to the 1986 World Cup Finals. It was also the night Jock Stein died

Jock Stein's death affected Davie badly.

The player had enormous respect for the manager and when Scotland finally made it through to the World Cup finals after a play-off against Australia Coop admitted simply: 'We did it for Jock'.

But if Davie had massive respect and admiration for Jock Stein the same certainly couldn't be said for the Scottish football set-up. Maybe that's understandable because our leagues have never exactly encouraged skill to flourish although there have been exceptions over the years.

The great Celtic team of the 1960s rose above the mediocrity that surrounded them with players like Jimmy Johnstone, Bertie Auld, Bobby Lennox and company showing how the game should be played. The Rangers team that included Coop himself, Bobby Russell and Gordon Smith was better than it was ever given credit for and the successful Aberdeen and Dundee United sides of the Alex Ferguson and Jim McLean eras had plenty of players who could play. In the present day too, Brian Laudrup has shone like a beacon since arriving in this country.

But overall Coop painted a pretty dismal picture and he said more than once if it hadn't been for his family he would have been off. The continent would have welcomed him for sure but instead he chose to remain close to home even if it was sometimes against his better judgement.

The Premier League does nothing to encourage players with above-average skill and ability. I for one have never found it suits my style of play.

To be brutally frank, the Premier League is the last place I would advise players of real talent to pursue their careers for it's very seldom they are given a chance to actually *play* and I find that sad. After all, the game is meant to be about entertainment but our entertainment is different from anywhere else. Not many world-class players would survive in our League where there are as many hammer-throwers as there are players. Basically, the Premier League kills class.

In Europe, guys get more time on the ball and therefore there is a greater chance of the finer points of the game flourishing. Not so here where a fair number of our matches are like the games we had at school when it was 32-a-side and everyone charged about like headless chickens. Not only that. They are really tall headless chicks and I sometimes wonder if a lot of our players are only in the game because they are over six foot tall. It leaves me a bit frustrated.

We get the occasional top-class player but it's about as regular as a sighting of Haley's Comet and it's no wonder we struggle to field exceptional players in the international squad.

WE CAN NEVER BE AN INTERNATIONAL FORCE AS LONG AS THE SYSTEM DICTATES THAT STAMINA IS MORE IMPORTANT THAN SKILL, TENSION REPLACES TALENT AND KICKERS ARE REWARDED IN THE SAME WAY AS CLASS PLAYERS.

Davie hated all that, just as he disliked intensely the idea of teams playing each other four times a season:

Familiarity does breed contempt; feuds are carried over from game to game and when that happens there's even less chance of having a constructive 90 minutes.

Ironically, it was something Davie was determined to try and change. He never bragged that he could alter the system on his own but he *did* believe he had something to offer younger players.

He was in the throes of setting up a coaching school at Clydebank and, of course, was actively involved in helping youngsters when he tragically collapsed at Clyde's Broadwood Stadium.

He managed to put something back into the game in a relatively short space of time but there was so much, so very much, more he could have done.

JIM BETT

Davie was born just 100 yards or so from where I lived in Hamilton so I suppose it was inevitable we would become close pals. Yet it wasn't really till I joined Rangers that I got to know him well.

Obviously, I knew all about him because he was a big name but I had never played alongside him till Ibrox. Then we hit it off on and off the park very quickly. We just seemed to know what one another would do and when we would do it. It worked a treat for Rangers and, indeed, Scotland when we played for the national side together.

I remember a famous win over Spain when the whole team played well but for Davie and me everything we touched seemed to come off. We both played particularly well that night. And there's no doubt in my mind he should have won far more than 22 caps for the country.

There was no point whatsoever in trying to teach tactics to Davie because, apart from anything else, he wasn't really interested. But, more seriously, you didn't need to anyway because it took just a few seconds of magic from him and a game could be turned on its head. He could always produce something unexpected that no one could cater for. It must have been a nightmare for defenders trying to mark him because, although quite a few could probably match him for pace, not one could match him for skill. Not many people could.

He was certainly as good as any top European name you care to mention. He was a magnificent servant to Rangers most of all but also to Motherwell and Clydebank.

I think his best spell, though, came after Graeme Souness took over as manager of Rangers. Davie was all of a sudden surrounded by better players and he responded in some style. Graeme knew he could play as well and that gave Davie a lot of confidence.

He played some outstanding football for 'Gers in the couple of years after Souness took over.

Away from football there's no doubt he liked his private life to be just that – private. He left Ibrox after training and generally headed straight to the bookies for a couple of hours. But the older he got the more he came out of his shell and from not really having anything to do with the media he all of a sudden was comfortable with newspapermen and television people. I think it had something to do with them being on his side in a contract battle with Rangers! He became so comfortable with it all that he looked set for a career in television after he finished with football.

But he would certainly never have had a career in cleaning if the hotel rooms we shared around the world were anything to go by. We roomed together when we were away with Scotland especially and it's fair to say the room was just a bit untidy. Ironically, we were sharing when we both experienced one of the major disappointments of our careers.

It was at the World Cup in Mexico in 1986 and both of us had played really well during the qualifying games. We reckoned we had done our bit to help Scotland to the finals so when we weren't involved much in Mexico it was a very real disappointment. To be honest, we both got a bit frustrated.

Manager Alex Ferguson wanted to try something a bit different tactically and it meant we were left out. Davie, I think, managed a couple of substitute appearances but I never got a kick in anger. So it was maybe just as well we roomed together because we could console each other. It would have been a good stage for Coop too.

However, it wasn't to be and the funny thing was he then went back home and had that great spell for Rangers.

There's no doubt, though, that he could have gone and played football anywhere. He was that good. The biggest problem with Davie was that when you took him out of Hamilton he was lost.

With a no doubt well-deserved Younger's Tartan Special player of the month award

TOMMY CRAIG

The memory of Davie Cooper's death will be with Tommy Craig forever. The Aberdeen coach was with Coop the day he collapsed at Broadwood back in March.

It was desperate. Coop was taken from us in a matter of seconds and even now I can't comprehend that. The medical people have tried to explain to me how that happens but I still don't understand it. Davie was there one second – ironically taking one of his favourite free kicks – and the next he was gone.

It was an awful, tragic, terrible moment.

The duo, together with Celtic's Charlie Nicholas, were doing a coaching course that was being televised by Scottish Television when the tragedy happened.

There was nothing untoward to suggest anything at all was wrong with Davie. He was as bright and bubbly as ever. There was no warning, no signal that anything was wrong. He had been so good with the youngsters at Broadwood. He had built up a camaraderie with the 16 kids in the group.

There were 12 boys and four girls and they were always laughing and joking with Davie. He had that kind of effect on people and he made them all feel at ease. They loved him for it but that was a kind of private side to him that not everyone knew or saw. I must admit that it was a side of him I didn't know either until I became a friend.

I had always had an impression of him as being fairly withdrawn and shy and quiet. A guy who just went about and did his own business. But at that Soccer Skills Course I got an insight into him and he was a very funny man. You had to get to know him before you appreciated that. But he was actually fairly outgoing and great company.

He was particularly good with the kids whom he got to know very well on that course. And it was his humour that shone through all the time. He and Charlie Nicholas were on the same wavelength when it came to practical jokes and wind-ups. The youngsters loved him for it all and every morning we went in they would want to know if Davie was there yet. They all took it very badly.

Everyone did, of course, but if Craig found a new side to Coop on that course he had his views about Davie's skill and ability merely reinforced.

When I came back to Scotland after 15 years in England my third game for Hibs was against Rangers and it was the first time I had seen Davie at close quarters. I had seen him on television, of course, but this was a first-hand view. And when I watched him I honestly felt he could have played in Brazil or anywhere else in the world. I don't like over-stating anything but Davie had the talent to play anywhere.

A lot of people have talked about his control and that was wonderful but for me it was his vision that was his greatest asset. Davie could actually see a move when there were five stages still to go. He could see the beginning and end of a move at the one time. He wasn't just a winger – he was a footballer.

He wasn't the quickest in terms of pace but he was the quickest thinker I've ever seen. He saw things so much earlier than anyone else. And he simply loved to create goals for others. I remember one he set up for Ian Durrant and even before the ball was in the net he had turned away to salute the crowd as if to say: 'I know Durranty is going to score but that was *my* goal.'

He was a wonderful player.

CHARLIE NICHOLAS

Charlie Nicholas stood side by side with Davie Cooper on the fateful day in March. The duo — one-time Old Firm rivals — were filming, together with Tommy Craig, a Scottish Television football skills series called Shoot.

They had become close friends during the recordings at Clyde's Broadwood Stadium in Cumbernauld. Just seconds before Davie collapsed the pair had been talking about going for a beer that evening. The Celtic star recalls:

He was happy and relaxed then the next thing I realised was that he had fallen back. The kids on the course thought he was clowning around but, of course, he was so desperately ill. It was awful.

His friend's death the following day affected Nicholas badly as it did so very many people. But gradually through the pain and sadness of that sudden loss Charlie has tried to concentrate on the multitude of great memories of a marvellous footballer. He continues:

There's still sadness, of course, but when I think about Davie I have so many happy memories that it makes me smile a little.

Coop had a special genius which made him stand out from others. He just loved playing the game and making football fans smile.

We always knew each other from our footballing days and we did have a lot of respect for each other. But during the recording of *Shoot* we became good mates and shared a lot of laughs. You could see how much Davie enjoyed helping the kids. He was what football should be all about.

When I looked at some of the Celtic reserves, they looked as if they had a burden on their back and that shouldn't be the case at that stage of their careers. Football should be fun but it's far too serious and that's partly why the game in Scotland can be so mediocre. Davie made football fun and that shone through every time you watched him.

Apart from his football ability which was second to none he was also one of the most down to earth guys you could wish to meet.

He lived and breathed football and away from it if he had a fiver in his pocket he was quite happy. He didn't ask or want for much more. Davie wasn't the type of person who was into the glamorous side of life.

To be honest, there's not a day goes past when I don't think about him. His death was so shocking.

Charlie, naturally, was one of the thousands of people who paid their last respects at Davie's funeral in Hamilton. When he turned up to say a final goodbye it almost became too much for him to handle.

I was walking up to the church with a red, white and blue wreath under my arm, the crowds at both sides just seemed to open up in front of me and it was like walking a gauntlet.

It was the most incredible feeling of my life because everywhere I looked there was a sea of faces. Men, women, kids in tears. It was very emotional and when I handed the wreath to a steward he looked at me and asked me if I was OK. I was so choked I couldn't even manage a reply.

They say time is the great healer but Charlie Nicholas still finds it hard to come to terms with Davie's death. Yet he takes comfort from all those memories and from his belief that Davie was 'a football magician – a one-off'.

He borrowed from elsewhere a tribute that he personally believes sums up Davie Cooper: 'His life was a celebration of football'.

TOM BOYD

Davie Cooper was, quite simply, the most gifted player I have ever played alongside. He could do things with a ball that us lesser mortals could only dream about. He had such amazing skill and ability.

Davie always enjoyed scoring goals but he loved even more to help others. He liked to set up goals for team-mates but he also got a great thrill from just setting up a good move by bringing others into the game. I think everyone who ever played alongside him would go along with that.

He knew that if you were prepared to make the runs then he would put the ball wherever you wanted it. It was a tremendous gift. Certainly, it was that attribute that helped my own career enormously. He was a huge influence on me when we were together at Motherwell. There's no doubt that he helped shape my career. And it's absolutely remarkable to think back to what he did for Motherwell.

If Graeme Souness was behind what they called the Rangers' revolution then Davie Cooper was behind the transformation of Motherwell. He was, first and foremost, the difference between Motherwell being an ordinary club and a reasonably successful one. Some people thought he went to Fir

Park to wind down after his glory years at Ibrox but that simply wasn't the case. Davie was still a great player and the fact that he was prepared to go to 'Well definitely improved the club's image. It lifted the stature of the place and the fact that someone of his pedigree and ability was there undoubtedly put more belief into the existing players.

I don't think, for instance, that Motherwell would have won the Scottish Cup in 1991 if Davie hadn't joined the club. And I think that one game, that one success, proved a point for him.

He didn't want people to think he had gone out to grass at Fir Park and the fact that he helped us win the Cup left him believing he had proved his point. Not that he really needed to because everyone must have known about his ability and, for that matter, the pride he took in his own performance.

Opposite: Goooooooooaaaaaaaaaalllll . . . !

PETER GRANT

I discovered just how much of an impact Davie Cooper had made on Scottish football when I found myself in danger of missing the 1995 Tennents Scottish Cup Final.

Don't get me wrong, I knew long before then that he was a great player. After all, he had done Celtic some damage over the years. But when I was injured playing for Celtic against Dundee United a fortnight before the Cup final I was sure, along with thousands of others, that I would miss the big day. I had ligament trouble and that normally takes a whole lot longer than two weeks to clear up, so I was pretty down in the dumps at the time. Yet what heartened me as much as anything and what gave me the will and desire to battle to try and get fit for the Hampden clash with Airdrie were the letters of support I received from Rangers fans. And I believe Coop was the man behind that.

He was probably the only player who has been able to cross the great divide in Glasgow. Unfortunately, it took his tragic death to unite supporters but what a legacy to leave.

Some of those same fans united once more to wish me well in my

At a charity fund-raising event with Celtic's Peter Grant and model Laura King

recovery from injury. As it happens, I made it for the final thanks, in a way, to Coop.

CHAPTER SIX

Caps and Coop

Davie Cooper started out on the international trail with Scotland at Under-18 level. But it was really when he burst onto the Under-21 scene in 1976 that he first captured the spotlight.

His first cap at that age group came against Czechoslovakia when he was with Clydebank. This was the Scottish line-up: Clark, Burley, Stanton, Aitken, Albiston, Wark, Narey, Burns, Cooper, McNiven, Sturrock.

Score: Czechoslovakia 0, Scotland 0.

Next up was Wales in February 1977.

Team: Clark, Burley, Albiston, Ross, Reid, Aitken, Cooper, Wark, Burns, Parlane, Sturrock.

Score: Scotland 3 (Wark, Sturrock, McNiven *sub*), Wales 2.

The following month the young Scots travelled to Switzerland. *Team*: Clark, Burley, Narey, Reid, Albiston, Wark, Cooper, Aitken, Hartford, Melrose, Sturrock.

Score: Switzerland 2, Scotland 0.

And in the April the babes faced England. *Team*: Ferguson, Sinclair, Stevens, Reid, Watson, McGarvey, Cooper, Burns, Fitzpatrick, Craig, Sturrock.

Score: England 1, Scotland 0.

Coop played in those four Under-21 fixtures as a Bankies player and after joining Rangers he won two further caps at that level against Switzerland and Czechoslovakia again. *Team v* the Swiss on 7 September 1977 was: Stewart, Burley, Albiston, Miller, Narey, Fitzpatrick, Sturrock, Payne, Wallace, Burns, Cooper.

Score: Scotland 3 (Wallace 2, Cooper), Switzerland 1.

The side against the Czechs later that month was: Stewart, Burley, Albiston, Miller, Narey, Fitzpatrick, Sturrock, Payne, McGarvey, Aitken, Cooper.

Score: Scotland 2 (Burley, Sturrock), Czechoslovakia 1.

Opposite: Before a Scotland game against Spain

A lot of those names, like Coop, went on to full international honours. Davie, in fact, had to wait until September 1979 for his call-up to the senior squad.

That first selection would have been honour enough but the fact that the manager of the time was the legendary Jock Stein made the occasion even more special. The game was a Hampden friendly against Peru. This was the Scotland line-up on Coop's international debut: Rough, Jardine, Munro, Souness, McQueen, Burns, Cooper, Aitken, Dalglish, Hartford, Robertson. Substitute: Wark for Cooper.

Score: Scotland 1 (Robertson), Peru 1.

Next time out was the following month and a European Championship clash with Austria. Coop, on this occasion, was a substitute. *Team*: Rough, Jardine, McQueen, Burns, Munro, Souness, Wark, Gemmill, Graham, Dalglish, Robertson. Substitute: Cooper for Graham.

Score: Scotland 1 (Gemmill), Austria 1.

Those two games weren't much to show for some fine form at the time. But they were all Coop got until he managed to bridge the long gap – four years – by returning to the international fold against Wales in February 1984. It had been a long and frustrating wait for the winger who, to be fair, had had his problems at club level. But he welcomed the return to the Scotland squad and marked his recall with a goal.

The personnel had changed a bit too. *Team v* Wales: Leighton, Gough, Albiston, Souness, McLeish, Miller, Sturrock, McStay, McGarvey, Bett, Cooper. Substitutes: Aitken for McStay, Johnston for McGarvey.

Score: Scotland 2 (Cooper, Johnston), Wales 1.

Then it was the big one against the Auld Enemy England at Hampden and a chance for Davie to pit his wits against defenders like Kenny Sansom and one Graham Roberts!

Aside from those two, there were some other quality players in the English ranks at the time. Ray Wilkins strutted his stuff in the middle of the park alongside Bryan Robson and Tony Woodcock and Luther Blissett were around as well. But this was the Scots side: Leighton, Gough, Albiston, Wark, McLeish, Miller, Strachan, Archibald, McGhee, Bett, Cooper. Substitutes: McStay for Strachan, Johnston for McGhee.

Score: Scotland 1 (McGhee), England 1.

The following season Coop played three more games. The first was against Yugoslavia and the team was: Leighton, Nicol, Albiston, Souness,

With Maurice Johnston and Jim Leighton

McLeish, Miller, Dalglish, Wark, Johnston, Bett, Cooper. Substitutes: Sturrock for Dalglish, McStay for Wark, Nicholas for Cooper.

Score: Scotland 6 (Souness, Dalglish, Sturrock, Johnston, Cooper, Nicholas), Yugoslavia 1.

That was an impressive result and performance and the Scots kept it going the following month – October – against Iceland. *Team*: Leighton, Nicol, Albiston, Souness, McLeish, Miller, Dalglish, McStay, Johnston, Bett, Cooper. Substitute: Nicholas for Dalglish.

Score: Scotland 3 (Souness, McStay 2), Iceland 0.

Scotland were on a roll and Davie was certainly playing his part in

Above: Eyes down, look in and that spells danger to the opposition

Opposite: Mixing with the best and this time it's Germany's Karl-Heinz Rummenigge

proceedings. They went into a double header against Spain in November '84 and February '85 in good spirits.

In the first game in Glasgow the Scots produced a devastating display with this side: Leighton, Nicol, Albiston, Souness, McLeish, Miller, Dalglish, McStay, Johnston, Bett, Cooper.

Score: Scotland 3 (Dalglish, Johnston 2), Spain 1.

It was one of the memorable Scotland performances – but it wasn't quite matched in the return in Seville. *Team*: Leighton, Gough, Miller, McLeish, Albiston, McStay, Bett, Souness, Cooper, Archibald, Johnston. Substitutes: Strachan for McStay, Nicholas for Archibald.

Score: Spain 1, Scotland 0.

Next was Wales again and the line-up for the Glasgow clash was: Leighton, Nicol, Albiston, McLeish, Miller, McStay, Dalglish, Souness, Cooper, Bett, Johnston. Substitutes: Hansen for Albiston, Nicholas for McStay.

Score: Scotland 0, Wales 1.

Coop's next appearance was in September 1985 in yet another game against Wales that will always be remembered for things other than his winning penalty. It was, of course, the night Jock Stein died. And, really, that made the Scots victory – important though it was – totally meaningless.

The team on that tragic occasion was: Leighton, Gough, Malpas, Aitken, McLeish, Miller, Nicol, Strachan, Sharp, Bett, Speedie. Substitutes: Rough for Leighton, Cooper for Strachan.

Score: Wales 0, Scotland 1 (Cooper penalty).

East Germany was next. *Team*: Leighton, Gough, Albiston, Souness, McLeish, Miller, Dalglish, Nicol, Johnston, Aitken, Cooper. Substitutes: Goram for Leighton, Speedie for Johnston, McStay for Aitken.

Score: Scotland 0, East Germany 0.

After that it was another double whammy – this time against Australia – as Scotland battled to get through to the World Cup finals in Mexico.

The first game was, fortunately, in Glasgow in November 1985. *Team*: Leighton, Nicol, Malpas, Souness, McLeish, Miller, Dalglish, Strachan, McAvennie, Aitken, Cooper. Substitute: Sharp for Dalglish.

Score: Scotland 2 (McAvennie, Cooper), Australia 0.

Opposite: Davie with Celtic stars Roy Aitken and Paul McStay and the lucky mascot before the World Cup qualifying ties against Australia

That was the job more or less done although the Scots had still to weather a Melbourne storm just a couple of weeks later. *Team* Down Under was: Leighton, Gough, Malpas, McLeish, Miller, Aitken, McAvennie, Souness, McStay, Speedie, Cooper. Substitute: Sharp for Speedie.

Score: Australia 0, Scotland 0.

It was a good season for Coop at the highest level and he continued to be an integral part of the Scotland side.

The following April the international side met Holland in Eindhoven and this was the team: Goram, Malpas, Albiston, Narey, McLeish, Miller, Sturrock, Bett, McCoist, Connor, Cooper.

Score: Holland 0, Scotland 0.

And so to the World Cup in far-off Mexico. Coop was left out entirely as the Scots lost 1–0 to Denmark in their opening game. But he was on the bench next time round against West Germany in the section that became known as the 'Group of Death'. *Team* against the Germans was: Leighton, Gough, Malpas, Souness, Narey, Miller, Strachan, Aitken, Nicol, Archibald, Bannon. Substitutes: McAvennie for Nicol, Cooper for Bannon.

Score: Scotland 1 (Strachan), West Germany 2.

After that game in Queretaro it was back to Nezahualcoyotl where they had played their first game for the next match against Uruguay. Once again Davie was on the bench – but maybe he was safer there, for a while at least. The Uruguayans, later labelled 'scum' by the Scottish Football Association's Ernie Walker, had a man sent off after *54 seconds* and that set the tone for a vicious match.

The side that battled against all the odds for Scotland was: Leighton, Gough, Albiston, Aitken, Narey, Miller, Strachan, McStay, Sharp, Nicol, Sturrock. Substitutes: Cooper for Nicol, Nicholas for Sturrock.

Score: Uruguay 0, Scotland 0.

So Scotland bowed out of the World Cup – battered, bewildered and bloody furious.

'Jose Batista was sent off for a horrendous foul on Gordon Strachan,' recalled Davie later. 'And that set the pattern for a ferocious series of assaults on the lads. By the time I went on it was patently obvious it would take a miracle rather than just me to manage a goal against them.

'I'm the first to admit we didn't play well anyway but how can you when you're chopped at every turn? The Uruguayans weren't going to concede anything that day come hell or high water.'

A thoughtful moment

Relaxing by the pool with Scotland pal Gordon Durie

Opposite: A rare photograph – Coop heading the ball and in an international at that

It was a disappointing end to what had, though, been a roller-coaster campaign from the start of qualifying to the finish in Nezahualcoyotl. But it was by no means the end of Davie's international career. He picked up the threads again just a few months after the World Cup against Bulgaria. This was the side: Leighton, Gough, Malpas, McStay, Narey, Miller, Cooper, Aitken, Johnston, Strachan, Nicholas. Substitute: Dalglish for Nicholas.

Score: Scotland 0, Bulgaria 0.

Coop then missed a game against the Republic of Ireland away before returning for a clash with Luxembourg. *Team*: Leighton, Stewart, MacLeod, Aitken, Gough, Hansen, Nevin, McClair, Johnston, Dalglish, Cooper. Substitutes: McCoist for MacLeod, McStay for Hansen.

Score: Scotland 3 (Johnston, Cooper 2, one penalty), Luxembourg 0.

But in typical Scotland fashion, a good result was followed by a nightmare and when the Republic of Ireland visited Glasgow it turned out to be a bit of a disaster. *Team*: Leighton, Stewart, Malpas, McCoist, Gough, Hansen, Nevin, McClair, Johnston, Strachan, Cooper. Substitutes: Aitken for McCoist, McStay for Cooper.

Score: Scotland 0, Republic of Ireland 1.

A couple of months – and games – later and Davie was back in business. And against Brazil of all countries. The game at Hampden followed hard on the heels of a 0–0 draw against England. *Team*: Goram, Gough, MacLeod, Aitken, McLeish, Miller, McStay, McInally, McCoist, Wilson, Cooper. Substitute: McClair for McInally.

Score: Scotland 0, Brazil 2.

That was to be Davie's last international appearance as a Rangers player and, to most judges, his last for Scotland full stop. Few people, if any, believed he could play again for his country after leaving Rangers for Motherwell. But Coop delighted in proving all the sceptics wrong and not for the first time he had the last laugh on the alleged experts who had written him off.

Amazingly, he was recalled to the Scotland squad for a crucial World Cup qualifying match against Norway in 1989 and he managed one more appearance after that – against Egypt. The line-up against the Norwegians in Glasgow was: Leighton, McPherson, Malpas, Aitken, McLeish, Miller, Johnston, McStay, McCoist, Bett, Cooper. Substitutes: MacLeod for Miller, McClair for Cooper.

Score: Scotland 1 (McCoist), Norway 1.

And then, finally, it was Egypt in a Pittodrie friendly. *Team*: Gunn, McKimmie, Gough, Gillespie, McLeish, Malpas, Bett, McStay, Cooper, Durie, McCoist. Substitutes: McCall for McKimmie, Levein for McLeish.

Score: Scotland 1 (McCoist), Egypt 3.

It was an ignominious end to a first-class international career, but the over-riding question remains. How did Coop win only 22 caps for Scotland?

CRAIG BROWN

Scotland boss Craig Brown was a long-time admirer of Davie Cooper's skills and he declared:

I rated him at least equal to the very best.

But if Brown's admiration knew no bounds he recalls the fact that it wasn't a view shared by an acquaintance of his many years ago. And his story explains exactly why Davie, born and bred in Hamilton, was never picked up by Motherwell Football Club at an early age.

Brown remembers that Fir Park blunder well.

Willie McLean was Motherwell manager at the time and I was his assistant. We were desperate to sign a left-sided midfield man or winger to complete the jigsaw in what we felt was a good 'Well side. So we despatched a scout to watch Davie play for Clydebank.

In fact, the scout actually went to see Coop play three times and eventually came back to us with his verdict. He gave us his report on the player in the form of a kind of checklist. On it were a number of headings with comments at the side. It was something like this:

Davie Cooper (Clydebank)

Heading ability – not very impressive

Tackling – simply can't tackle

Pace – moderate

Right-foot – almost non-existent

Left-foot – good

Now, when we looked at that the only conclusion we could come to was that Davie wasn't the answer for us because it didn't make very inspired reading. But it also shows just how inaccurate a checklist can be!

That 'good' left foot was really all Davie needed to go on and become a tremendous player. He simply didn't need to be good at any of the rest of the aspects of the game.

I then recall him going on to become an excellent player for the Bankies and, of course, for Rangers, Motherwell and indeed Scotland.

But it was really only in 1986 that Brown studied Coop at close quarters.

We were at the World Cup in Mexico where I was part of then manager Alex Ferguson's backroom team. Training used to give me a good insight into the players and you could really only marvel at Davie's ability.

Ironically, Fergie only played him as substitute and against Uruguay in the last game he used Davie as the last throw of the dice with the score 0–0. Unfortunately, even Coop couldn't help Scotland to the all-important goal but he did very well.

The stay out there also let me get to know Davie better. He was a great character and the one thing that struck me was that *everyone* liked him.

But there was another fine example of the esteem in which Coop was held.

The setting was four years on and again it was time for the World Cup.

On this occasion the venue was to be Italy and Davie was playing so well – with Motherwell by then – that Andy Roxburgh and assistant Brown simply couldn't ignore him.

Not that we wanted to. In fact, Davie was always one of Andy's favourite players. But Davie injured himself preparing for the whole shooting match and he was such an honest guy that he was totally up front with Andy about the problem. Not every player would have admitted there was a doubt over his fitness. But Davie did and he explained to Andy that he didn't think he could possibly be ready for the first game against Costa Rica. He felt he would be OK for the next one against Sweden but Andy was concerned about it all.

In the end Andy decided that it was all too much of a risk and that we couldn't take Davie. Both the manager and the player were disappointed. Yet, Davie must have known his honesty could cost him caps and, for that matter, a fair bit of money plus the chance to play in another World Cup. He still elected to explain it all thoroughly and he took great credit from that, but it was also Scotland's loss.

He was such a good player and that in so many ways would have been the perfect stage for him.

But it wasn't to be although that late withdrawal from the World Cup squad was by no means Davie's last brush with the big-time. He continued to be a tremendous player for Motherwell.

He shone like a beacon at Fir Park, he was so good for the club and for players like Phil O'Donnell and Rob McKinnon.

Phil made those great runs of his from the middle of the park sure and confident in the knowledge that they wouldn't be wasted. Davie, inevitably, would play the perfect ball through and Phil would be on his way.

Really, Coop's every movement had sheer class stamped all over it. Those two guys have gone on to better things but I'm sure they would be the first to pay tribute to Coop and admit exactly how much they owe to one of Scotland's greatest-ever players.

This country doesn't unearth all that many genuinely world-class stars, but Coop came into that category without a shadow of a doubt.

CHAPTER SEVEN

Davie's All-time Greats

Players far and wide paid generous tributes to Davie when he died in March. They were given genuinely and sincerely because his fellow professionals recognise skill and ability before anyone else.

They had enjoyed playing in the same era as Coop and felt privileged they had been part of it all. Team-mates and opponents alike joined forces as one after the other recalled his favourite memory.

Many of them – and more – are involved in this book. Coincidentally, many were also favourites of Davie's and in *True Blue* he named his own cast of all-time greats.

It's worth recalling some of the players who figured in Coop's 'Hall of Fame'. The list from his beloved Ibrox is lengthy but in it are some of the greatest players ever to wear the famous jersey. Here they are and in no particular order with Coop's own fond memories.

GRAEME SOUNESS: He is a world-class player. He has the kind of arrogance associated with the old-time gunslingers and I think it's fair to say that there are players in the world genuinely scared of him.

He has a remarkable talent aided and abetted by an ability to take care of himself. Not many players can combine the two but he managed it very effectively. Few players do him for skill and equally few succeed in taking him on physically.

DEREK JOHNSTONE: There were few better in the country than DJ. He was, without doubt, the best header of a ball I have ever seen because he had the great ability to get up well and somehow hover before powering the ball away with the merest nod of his head. He was a winger's dream to play alongside because he turned bad crosses into good ones.

TOM FORSYTH: Fans identified him as a big, hard man but he's a softie really. Tam insisted on approaching training and playing as if his life depended on it.

He is best remembered for a marvellous tackle on Mick Channon that prevented a certain goal in the 1976 Scotland-England international but there is really so much more to him than that.

BOBBY RUSSELL: He's built like an X-ray but is stronger than many people imagine. Not that strength was his game, rather it was his delicate skill that did so much for Rangers. Considering that he went straight into the team from junior football the impact he made was remarkable. He and I shared an almost telepathic understanding. He knew exactly what I was doing and vice versa and the partnership worked a treat.

JOHN McCLELLAND: The big Irishman was a tremendous signing when he arrived for £90,000 from Mansfield Town as a virtual unknown. By anyone's standards that was a good bit of business.

He was a tremendous inspiration and captain at the club and was badly missed when he left for Watford.

JIM BETT: I only met him for the first time in the Ibrox dressing-room the day he signed for Rangers but from that minute our Hamilton backgrounds ensured we became close friends.

What a smashing player he is! We have played together for club and country and it has been a pleasure for me to be alongside him. He was the only other player – apart from Bobby Russell – with whom I had a complete understanding on the park.

TED McMINN: Big, daft Ted could be a world-beater one day and the next – or even later the same day! – he would look as if he had never been introduced to a football.

They broke the mould after him and I never came across anyone quite like Ted. At his best he was absolutely brilliant and at his worst, well, he was appalling.

There was never a dull moment with Ted around!

ALLY McCOIST: He's a dressing-room clown who occasionally borders on lunacy. But he's a great guy to have there because he's the same all the time.

He's a flamboyant character who tried hard not to let anything get him down and if he wasn't a footballer then I reckon he would be a singer. He does a 'rap' song that is nothing short of sensational and it's a party piece he has perfected through the years.

But Ally can play into the bargain. He came through a period when he got some stick from supporters but he answered all the critics by doing what he does best – scoring goals – and had the last laugh.

CHRIS WOODS: When you talk about keepers – wherever they are in the world – you tend to think about any flaws they have. The trouble with Chris is that he hasn't got any. He is good in the air, has terrific positional sense and seems to dominate the goal.

He's a quiet lad but I've worked out why. It's because he's speechless at the number of goals Ally McCoist and I knock past him in training every day.

TERRY BUTCHER: He is quite simply the best defender I have ever seen. In fact, he is the defence.

He could be a back four on his own he's so good and he just doesn't seem to have a weakness. He's got a great touch for a big man, he's virtually unbeatable in the air and he can play great passes out of defence to the front men. The opposition must look at Tel and wonder how on earth they're going to get the better of him.

He's also club captain and it's impossible to think of anyone better equipped for the job.

He has the respect of all the lads, is vastly experienced and is a magnificent ambassador for Rangers on and off the field.

Others who received honourable mentions included Ian Durrant, Derek Ferguson, Jimmy Nicholl, John Greig and Graham Roberts. But Davie was never so insular that he couldn't also appreciate the ability of players outwith Ibrox.

Clydebank's Jim Fallon was one and there were others from different clubs.

JIM FALLON: He was known as Mr Consistency and that tells you something about his attributes. Every game, every performance was the same. Nothing varied. He was the epitome of consistency.

WILLIE MILLER: He has shown tremendous loyalty to the Dons and he is a terrific player who has an enviable record of consistency at club and country levels.

You can always rely on Willie to be there when you most need him and while I have always admired that when he's in a Scotland jersey there are times when I could have done without it at club level!

Willie, in addition, is as good a referee as I have ever seen or heard.

Another Aberdeen star who impresses me is **STEWART MCKIMMIE** who I reckon is a very good player. I always find him a difficult opponent and he's a helluva man for making forward runs all the time.

ALAN ROUGH at Hibs just seems to stand in the middle of his goal and become a magnet for the ball.

But of all the players mentioned – and one not yet spoken about – only two stand out. One is the aforementioned Graeme Souness and the other is **KENNY DALGLISH**. He was an absolute joy to play alongside and I'm glad I can say I played in the same team as him a few times. He was a maestro of a player who seemed to know instinctively exactly what to do with the ball for the best.

It irritated me a bit when folk would look at his international record and say: 'He's got all those caps but he's only really played well in a handful of matches.' If that was the case then just about every good judge of football has been wrong over the years. He would be the first name down on any team sheet of mine.

All these players are British and although Davie never earned his living outside Scotland it didn't stop him admiring some of the best of the rest from around the world.

The names he trotted out read like a who's who of international football.

Here is his roll of honour from outside these islands.

HOLLAND: Arnold Muhren, Franz Thijssen; **ITALY**: Roberto Bettega, Alessandro Altobelli, Guiseppe Bergomi; **REPUBLIC OF IRELAND**: Liam Brady; **GERMANY**: Harald Schumacher, Bernd Schuster, Pierre Littbarski, Heinz Flohe, Hans-Peter Briegel, Klaus Allofs, Rainer Bonhof, Karl-Heinz Rummenigge; **ARGENTINA**: Diego Maradona, Mario

Kempes; **PORTUGAL**: Fernando Gomes; **DENMARK**: Morten Olsen, Soren Lerby, Frank Arnesen, Preben Elkjaer, Michael Laudrup; **BELGIUM**: Jean-Marie Pfaff, Eric Gerets, Franky van der Elst, Franky Vercautern, Rene Vandereycken, Enzo Scifo, Jan Ceulemans; **BRAZIL**: Josimar, Edinho, Junior, Socrates, Falcao, Zico, Casagrandes; **FRANCE**: Manuel Amoros, Patrick Battiston, Maxime Bossis, Bernard Genghini, Alain Giresse, Michel Platini, Jean Tigana, Yannick Stopyra; **SPAIN**: Zubizarreta, Maceda, Gallego, Victor, Caldere, Rincon, Butragueno, Carrasco; **RUSSIA**: Rinat Dasayev, Vladimir Bessonov, Alexander Chivadze, Anatoly Demyanenko, Vassili Rats, Igor Belanov.

That's a list of players Coop would have paid to watch if he hadn't been either alongside them or in opposition. The certainty about this is that he wasn't out of place among those names.

Coop – Lasting Memories

ALLY McCOIST

Ally McCoist was closer to Davie Cooper than most. It was natural, therefore, that Coop's death hit him hard and the Rangers striker was one of the first to visit the hospital where Davie lay and where, ultimately, he died.

Even now I find it difficult to believe he's gone. We were friends and team-mates for a long time and his death had an enormous effect on me. Obviously, in these circumstances you feel for his family and loved ones first and foremost. So many people were so devastated that it's clear his death has left an enormous gap in many, many lives. Coop was special. I had some great times with him on and off the park.

Some of those times were very public and millions of fans marvelled at the pair in tandem for Rangers and Scotland. Other moments were more private. But either way the duo were never far from a laugh and a joke.

One of the great moments of my career came after Davie had left Rangers for Motherwell. We had played against each other countless times when, one day, I struck oil! I actually got one over Davie with a piece of skill. Me, Ally McCoist did the great Davie Cooper with a little bit of magic. No wonder I remember it because it had never happened before.

I produced this little bit of genius when I dummied him and sent him completely the wrong way but really that only tells half the story. Immediately after I'd done him I felt down my sock and produced a complimentary ticket. 'Here,' I said as I handed it to Coop, 'That'll get you back in'. I'm not sure he saw the funny side of it at the time but we laughed long and hard about it afterwards. Anyway, I was entitled to one moment of glory. Coop, on the other hand, produced so many moments of pure magic everyone lost count.

There was something special in virtually every game he played and it was certainly a joy to be a team-mate although it must have been hell to be an opponent. That was even the case in training when we were together at Ibrox.

Davie wasn't the most enthusiastic trainer I ever came across but the one thing he did enjoy was a game among all the lads. We used to split into Scotland v England after the likes of Terry Butcher and Chris Woods arrived in Glasgow and Davie couldn't get enough of that action. It would be six or seven-a-side and the Scots team would include Davie, me, Ian Durrant, Robert Fleck and others. England would be made up of Butch, Chrissy, Graham Roberts etc. and we would clash every Friday. I'll tell you, we used to murder the English *every* time and we all loved it but no one more so than Coop.

He used to be ecstatic when we scored another famous victory over the Auld Enemy and although it happened all the time he never got bored with it. The games often had a little edge to them as you would expect but that suited Davie down to the ground and he danced past the English as if they weren't there. Big Tel and company got a bit frustrated at times. And their cause wasn't helped when Coop really rubbed salt into their wounds. He used to start taking the mickey eventually and he would actually commentate on the game as he was playing. We would fall around in stitches as we listened to him.

All we could hear was: 'Here's Cooper and he waltzes round Butcher, sets up McCoist and it's 3–0 to Scotland.' It would go on like that for ages and Coop loved every minute of the wind-ups. But Terry and the rest of the English lads took it well and they certainly had their eyes opened to Davie's talent.

I'm sure they knew a fair bit about Coop before they came north but they saw him in a different light when they played alongside him.

He was a genius.

Arguably, he was the most talented player this nation has ever seen. For me, he was definitely the best ever and there's no doubt that great players like big Butch developed an enormous respect for him.

Coisty, though, believes then manager Graeme Souness blundered badly when he let Coop go to Motherwell.

I know he was probably trying to do Davie a favour because he could no longer guarantee him anything like a regular place but I believe he sold him two years too soon. Rangers could have got that much longer out of Davie. After all, look what he did for the Fir Park club. He was never the quickest anyway so it wasn't as if he had lost a lot of pace. He was still a tremendous player when he left us and I honestly think it was too soon.

That saddens Ally and so, too, did the fact that Coop was only surrounded by genuine quality in the last couple of years of his glorious Rangers career.

That was a shame. He spent quite a long time playing in a Rangers side that wasn't that good and that was a bit of a waste. I think it was only after Souness arrived and lots of top stars ended up at Ibrox that he produced probably the best football of his career. There were special moments then.

I have never, for instance, seen a ball hit harder than the one he blasted past Jim Leighton in the Rangers-Aberdeen Skol Cup final in 1987–88. And seldom have I seen the kind of skill that took him past a handful of Ilves Tampere defenders in a European tie as he set up a goal for Flecky. I remember it so well. Coop danced past half their team and slipped the ball to Fleck. Coop was turning away to wave in triumph to the fans even before Robert scored!

He was involved in a fair amount of my goals as well although I could never quite understand why Davie liked setting them up as much as scoring himself. You would never find me admitting that!

Coop continued to weave his magic spell when he left Rangers for Motherwell. A lot of people thought his career would go into decline at that point but there was never any chance of that. Coop was too proud to let people think he had gone out to grass just because he had left his beloved Ibrox. He helped them win the Scottish Cup and I'm sure the Fir Park directors and officials as well as the players of the time would be the first to admit he helped put the club back on the map.

He did his bit in his second stint at Clydebank as well.

So many memories of so many magic moments it's no wonder Ally still finds it desperately hard to accept that Coop is no longer with us.

I feel cheated. Davie was ready to give so much back to the game he had graced for so long that it just wasn't fair.

I went to the Southern General the night he collapsed at Broadwood Stadium and then again the next day and it was all so desperately sad. Afterwards I went to Fir Park to see for myself the amazing tributes to him there and, of course, I made several trips to Ibrox.

On the Saturday and Sunday following his death there must have been 400 people around the gates constantly. You don't see grown men crying all that much but I saw plenty during that weekend. And I don't mind admitting I shed a lot of tears myself.

It was obviously a very difficult time but through it all I came to understand better than ever before just how much Coop had meant to people.

The floral tributes, the scarves, the jerseys, the flags were testimony to his popularity. And, surely, the fact that there were so many items put at those gates by fans of other clubs says it all.

He was a genuine great.

GRAEME CLARK

(WET WET WET)

Wet Wet Wet became heavily involved with Clydebank around the time Davie Cooper rejoined the Kilbowie club.

The popular group were among Coop's greatest fans. They took the opportunity to watch the Bankies' star whenever possible and the Rangers fans among them were given more opportunities to marvel at a talent they had seen often enough at Ibrox previously. Graeme Clark recalls:

Davie was one of *the* Rangers greats. Certainly, he was as good as any Ibrox star I have ever seen and watching him was watching someone special. You could only stand in awe of his genius.

Just about every Coop moment was magic but it must have been terrible for a defender facing him. The player might have seen Davie's tricks a dozen times before but he was still powerless to do anything about it. It was amazing.

But if it was a nightmare for defenders it was spectacular for team-mates and supporters alike. You would never tire of watching Davie. And there's no doubt in my mind that left foot of his could have opened a tin if he had wanted to! After all, it could do everything else.

The Wets, as entertainers, know a thing or two about pleasing fans and audiences and Graeme went on:

Davie was an entertainer too. I love my football but just as there are games that never rise above the ordinary so too there are players in the same boat. No one could ever say that about Coop. He was so very special to watch.

Clydebank twice, Rangers, Motherwell and Scotland were lucky to have his services. Fans everywhere – no matter who they support – were lucky to have seen him as well.

ROD STEWART

I never knew Davie Cooper that well. I certainly couldn't call myself a close friend but I was shocked by his death just like every other football fan. I still find it hard to believe he has gone.

I played against him in a charity match some years back up at Firhill. I reckon I matched him for speed, but that was about it. He was just so tricky he tied me up in knots.

That night I had nightmares and in every one I saw four Davie Coopers coming at me. But after that game he spent some time at the bar with me and I was really chuffed about that. I know Davie was never the greatest socialiser so for him to go out of his way like that was superb.

Like all the greats – Kenny Dalglish, Denis Law and the rest – he was an entertainer, the kind of guy you would really want to see play. I love wingers like Coop, Jinky Johnstone and even the young lad Brian McLaughlin at Celtic.

On stage, I love to put on a show because people want something different. There's no use me going on stage in jeans and singing from a bare platform – that would be like Davie playing right-back.

He knew how to put on a show and yet he was so underrated. I can never work out why he was capped so few times for Scotland.

GRAHAM CLARK

There have been many poignant moments during the writing of this book. It was always meant to be a tribute to one of Scotland's greatest players and a thoroughly nice man. Hopefully, the people I have spoken to about Coop reflect that.

There has been nothing but admiration for his skills and ability on the park, and nothing but friendship for him off it.

I could have spoken to thousands of other people who, I'm sure, would have had their own memories and recollections. But the cross-section of players, officials and managers I have talked to have been able to convey the thoughts of most others.

Inevitably, I will have missed someone out. Someone who has a particular incident or game or piece of magic they would like to have recalled. I'm sorry if that's the case.

Even now, some months after his tragic death, most people I have talked to still find it hard to come to terms with his passing. I certainly do.

There are, of course, constant reminders of his glorious life and career. I remember wondering exactly how a crowd of over 27,000 at Scott

Nisbet's Testimonial Match could remain quite so quiet during the minute's silence in Davie's memory. It was an astonishing tribute.

Similarly, at a game in aid of the *Daily Record* Davie Cooper Appeal at Pollok in June, there was not a murmur from the fans of all clubs who had gone along to see a star-studded match yet were silent during another moment to honour Coop. The same thing happened all over the country at various times.

There was nothing but respect for a great player.

There has been nothing but respect for a great man.

There is little more to add. Davie's untimely death left a huge gap in Scottish football and in so many lives. It will never be filled.

Following page: Davie's no longer with us and a nation mourned. His passing was felt most deeply in his native Hamilton, of course, and at Clydebank, Rangers and Motherwell where his glittering career was like a beacon. Fans paid remarkable tributes at Kilbowie, Ibrox and Fir Park and it was all too much for most people. This was the scene outside Ibrox

Above Charlie Nicholas pays a floral tribute

Right: Marti Pellow and Graeme Clark of Wet Wet Wet

Below: Celtic's Tom McAdam and manager Tommy Burns ahead of Steve Archibald

Above: The funeral in Hamilton was a day for everyone to pay their last respects and football superstars and the general public did just that. A tearful Ally McCoist and wife Allison can't contain their grief

Left: Alex Ferguson and Graeme Souness on their way to the service